the *Varsity*
guidebook to cambridge
city & university, written and
produced by cambridge students

cambridge
(through student eyes)

Editor and Publisher: Rachel Flowerday
Cover design: Rachel Flowerday
Cover photograph: Claude Schneider
Typeset in-house in Bookman and Gill Sans by
Rachel Flowerday and Tim Harris

Published by Varsity Publications Limited
11-12 Trumpington Street
Cambridge, CB2 1QA

Produced by Origen Production Limited
Printed and bound in Great Britain

ISBN 0-902240-30-7

First published 1991
Second edition 1993
Third edition 1997
Fourth edition 2000

contents

contents continued over page

contents continued

university city

historical cambridge

Before there was Gown, there was Town. There has been a settlement of sorts on the banks of the river Cam since Roman times. The bridge, from which the town takes its name, was built by Saxons in the 7th century.

After the Romans left, the river (known to the Saxons as the Granta, and today as the Cam) divided the kingdom of the mercians from that of the East Angles. The Saxons called the town Grantanbrycge; the Normans called it Grantebrigge; Chaucer called it Cantebrigge.

The river itself was the main source of the town's wealth; winding through the fens (the swampy marshland to the north of the town), it eventually joined the Ouse. Barges bringing goods from all over northwestern Europe stopped at Stourbridge (where a huge annual fair was held from July to September), Midsummer Common, and the Backs (the fields behind the colleges which run down to the river). Visitors gliding along the Backs in chauffeured punts are following the course taken by barges well into the 19th century. In the 18th century, one Master of Trinity College used to bring the produce of his rectory to his private granary on the river behind the college.

There is a long history of competition between the universities of Oxford and Cambridge, although when it comes to arguments over which is older it must sadly be admitted that Oxford probably has the advantage, the more fanciful inventions of generations of Cambridge scholars notwithstanding.

It is well documented that in 1209, following the killing of an Oxford student by some townsmen, the scholars went on strike. This was a serious business; in medieval times, the presence of a band of scholars in a town meant lucrative trade. The resulting diaspora of Oxford academics settled in several towns, but only in Cambridge did the settlement become permanent.

This immediately led to trouble. The scholars did not just bring their learning with them, but also their hostile attitude towards the townsfolk. Though the university was as yet unofficial, it assumed all the traditional rights of such a body. Conflicts grew increasingly fractious – one Chancellor even excommunicated the Mayor – and the University's hand was strengthened when in 1318, at the urging of Edward II, it was officially recognised by Pope John XXII.

Relations with townsfolk reached their lowest ebb in 1381, when a mob led by the Mayor and burgesses sacked most of the University buildings and burnt all the documents they could lay their hands on, with a cry of "away with the skills of the clerks!" Retribution for these acts was swift, and came in the form of the King granting the University control over many aspects of the life of the town, including the pricing of bread, wine and ale, the checking of weights and measures, and the licensing of entertainments – rights which the University retained until the 19th century.

The majority of the colleges, those communities which distinguish Oxford and Cambridge from most other universities, were founded in three waves. The first wave, founded from 1284 to 1352, were simply student halls of residence; St. Peter's (or Peterhouse) was the first, followed by Michael House and King's Hall (both of which later became parts of Trinity College), Clare Hall, Pembroke Hall, Gonville Hall, Trinity Hall and Bene't Hall (now Corpus Christi College). Many of these still survive, though only Peterhouse and Trinity Hall retain their original names; the rest have become known as colleges, or have been refounded under different designations.

The second wave occurred in the Tudor age, from 1441 (when King's College was founded) to 1596 (Sidney Sussex). Ironically, many of these colleges (Queens', Trinity, St. John's, Magdalene and Jesus) were built of red brick. The third wave has occurred over the last hundred years or so, and, reflecting the extensive changes which occurred in the University in the 19th century, includes the foundation of colleges for women and research students.

Like all medieval universities, Cambridge was home to scholars in all four of the great faculties: theology, medicine, law and the arts. Students wandered from university to university in search of the greatest teachers of the day; Cambridge was home to students from all over Europe. The Dutch scholar Erasmus, perhaps the greatest scholar of the Renaissance, taught at Queens' College between 1510 and 1513. He didn't enjoy it much, complaining incessantly about the cost of living in Cambridge (plus ça change), but he did like the women of the town, whom he called "divinely pretty, soft, pleasant, gentle, and charming as the Muses".

The conflicts that engulfed England over the next two hundred years were mirrored in Cambridge. During the 16th century, Cambridge became a hotbed of Protestantism, with many of her alumni being burnt at the stake for their faith in the 1530s and 1540s. Clashes between Papists and Protestants were a regular feature of University life through much of the century. One hundred years later, Cambridge was again rent in two, this time by Civil War; the division was along the by now traditional lines of Town (who supported Cromwell) and Gown (who supported the King, despite the fact that Cromwell was an alumnus of Sidney Sussex College). Not surprisingly, the University suffered under the Protectorate, but regained its position when Charles II was restored to the throne. This was also a period of great advancement of learning; to name but one participant in this process, Isaac Newton, discoverer of gravity, lived and worked at Trinity College.

The 18th century is commonly regarded as the nadir of the University's history, a period when students and scholars alike did little other than drink, gamble and carouse. It is certainly true that the energies of the University were not directed towards teaching, but this was because, as at no other time in the University's history, its affairs were intimately bound up with intrigue, influence, and all the other aspects of the new party politics. By the end of the century, however, the long neglect of its academic basis had begun to affect its reputation. Samuel Taylor Coleridge, who came up to Jesus College in 1791, wrote that "In Cambridge there are sixteen Colleges that look like workhouses, and fourteen churches that look like little houses. The town is very fertile in alleys, and mud, and cats, and dogs, besides men, women, ravens, clergy, proctors, tutors, owls, and other two-legged cattle."

A traveller from 1600 would have found much of the University of 1800 very familiar. The University's primary function was to educate young men who would enter the church; the study of mathematics was considered the best way of achieving this. By 1900, however, everything had changed. The town expanded and, with the coming of the railway in 1845, became more cosmopolitan. The University underwent enormous expansion, both in numbers of students and range of subjects taught. Students no longer had to be members of the Church of England. Extra-mural examinations were instigated. Lecture courses and examinations were opened to women. The traditional faculties were supplemented by laboratories of science, both pure and applied, teachers of multifarious languages both living and dead, and diverse new philosophies. All this change came under the influence of outside competition (the University of London was founded in the 1830s), outside scrutiny (Royal Commissions in the 1850s and 1870s), and a reforming instinct from within, which one historian has called 'the revolution of the dons'.

The changes set underway in the second half of the 19th century gathered pace at the beginning of this century. Burgeoning numbers of research students found a home in the University. The reputation of the University's scientific departments – particularly the Cavendish Laboratory and the Institute of Biochemistry – grew and grew, numerous Nobel Prizes being garnered by scientists educated or based in Cambridge. Women were finally admitted to degrees in 1947 and, in the 1970s, the colleges began to go mixed (the last all-male bastion being breached when Magdalene went mixed in 1988). Students campaigned for a voice in the academic affairs of the University; an effective University-wide Students' Union developed in the early 1970s.

It is easy to see Cambridge as a place of unchanging tradition, but this is far from the case. Today, at the dawn of the 21st century, the pace of change is rapid. New departments are being created, and old ones renovated, funded by a massive development appeal, to keep Cambridge at the fore-front of the academic world. The academic centre of gravity of the University, which has shifted over the centuries from the Old Schools, and is currently split between the Science area next to Downing Street and the Arts site on Sidgwick Avenue, is set to shift yet again, to West Cambridge, where green field sites are currently being developed for University use.

The Law Faculty

The History Faculty

the university today

Cambridge has no campus, but rather a collection of colleges and academic departments. All students are junior members of one of the 31 colleges (six colleges are devoted to graduates, and three are for women only). Many, but not all, of the University's academics are also fellows (senior members) of one of the colleges. The college is the centre of the undergraduate's life: it provides accommodation, food, individual tuition, pastoral care and entertainments (usually organised by the students themselves).

The departments are responsible for organising lectures and (where appropriate) practical work for undergraduates. Each department has its own library. The departments are grouped together into faculties; these bodies co-ordinate the teaching curriculum set examinations, and judge the quality of research submitted for advanced degrees.

The actual power of granting the degrees rests with the University, however, rather than with the colleges or departments. Degrees are awarded at a ceremony held several times a year at the Senate House on King's Parade. The largest of these ceremonies is the General Admission to BA degrees, spread over several days at the end of June, at which nearly all the final year undergraduates (some 3,000 in all) receive their degrees; by

The Senate House (left) faces Caius College (right)

a curious quirk of University tradition, all undergraduates receive BA (Bachelor of Arts) degrees, even if they have studied a scientific subject.

Behind the Senate House are the Old Schools. These buildings housed the faculties and the University Library until the early 19th century; they now contain the University's administrative centre. The University Library moved from this site in 1934 to its modern home across the river, the work of Giles Gilbert Scott. The Library is one of the country's five copyright libraries, entitled by law to a copy of any book published in this country. Whilst in practice the Library does not actually take every book, it does have an enormous collection of over 4 million volumes (many of which are very rare, or even unique), as well as extensive manuscript holdings.

A significant proportion of the books held in the University Library were published in Cambridge by the University Press. The Press dates back to 1534, when it was granted a charter by Henry VIII, and was once housed in the Pitt building on Trumpington Street, built in 1833 with the surplus from public subscriptions for a statue of William Pitt (Prime Minister 1783-1805). The Press has now moved most of its operations to new premises near the railway station. The church-like appearance of the Pitt building's façade led to its being dubbed 'the freshers' church', after the hoax played on generations of Cambridge freshmen who were informed that their presence was required there on the first Sunday of the academic year. Even today, one may spot the occasional bemused, gowned student outside the building on the second Sunday in October.

The University is a self-governing body. The position of Chancellor is, and has been for many centuries, largely ceremonial. Real influence rests with the Vice-Chancellor, who presides over the Council of Senate, which is made up of senior fellows of the University. The Council's proposals – known as 'graces' – are debated by the University's resident fellows. A vote is held upon a matter if, when the grace is read out, one of the fellows says "non placet" ('it does not please'). The reports of the Council of Senate and the graces are printed in the Cambridge University Reporter, the official University journal; although the Reporter is not supposed to carry any controversial material, it does have an 'unofficial' section, in which the often heated debates are closely reported. The Vice-Chancellor used to be a part-time job, held for two years by one of the Heads of the Colleges; due to recent changes in the University's administrative structure, the present incumbent, Professor Sir Alec Broers, is the second full-time Vice-Chancellor.

Discipline is maintained within the colleges by the Dean, who has the power to fine offenders as he sees fit. At a University level, the officials responsible for discipline are called 'proctors'. The job of proctor is today far less onerous, and far less dangerous, than in the past. In years gone by, the proctors would patrol the city's streets, wearing gown and mortar board, accompanied by two 'bulldogs' (burly porters who could catch, and restrain, unruly students) to check that students weren't frequenting undesirable hostelries, or committing the truly heinous crime of not wearing their gown.

literary cambridge

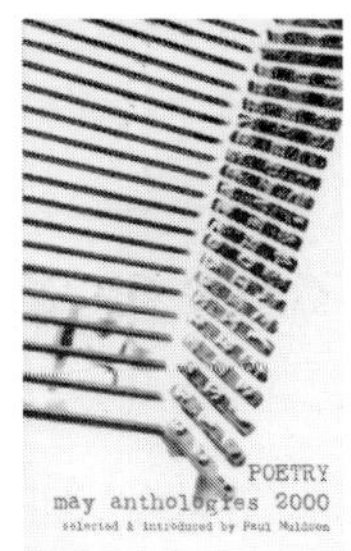

There's no end to writers in Cambridge – especially if you can see ghosts. Starting with Edmund Spenser, Thomas Grey, Christopher Smart and Ted Hughes at Pembroke, it's only a few yards before you trip over Christophers Marlowe and Isherwood at Corpus Christi, Henry James on King's Parade, and even – rumour has it – William Shakespeare at St. Johns... In truth, most of them hated Cambridge: Samuel Coleridge left to join the army under an assumed name, and Phillip Larkin vented his spleen in *Jill*, a novel to put any potential undergrad off for life. Some were happier, like E.M. Forster, who returned in his later years – mainly, it seems, to entice unwitting male undergrads to tea in his rooms! Perhaps he was remembering happier days, when the Bloomsbury set were happy and gay at Rupert Brooke's Vicarage in Grantchester. Virginia Woolf tells a remarkable story in her diary about Brooke's naked swimming exploits, proving that, in his case, it wasn't only the pen that was mighty...

If you like your writers a little more alive, both town and gown have a liberal scattering of writers – with a large Aussie contingent. Although Germaine Greer teaches at Warwick now, she can still be spotted in Cambridge... perhaps visiting old enemy Clive James, who lives by Jesus Green. *Stand* editor and Australian poet John Kinsella lives up at Churchill, and writers of all nationalities and persuasions pass through the town to give readings at colleges and bookshops. Most University and college events are open to the public: in 2000, you could have applauded Margaret Atwood's witticisms, admired Beryl Bainbridge's *Master Georgie* and heard academics such as Harold Bloom lecture on their latest books. Cambridge is home to writers as diverse as both publicity-hungry novelist Jeffrey Archer and reclusive poet JH Prynne.

The May Anthologies 2000: Short Stories (below) and Poetry (opposite)

SHORT STORIES
may anthologies 2000
selected & introduced by Lawrence Norfolk

But if you want your writers REALLY live, try cafés CB1 (Mill Road) and CB2 (Norfolk Street), which boast a full programme of readings and literary events. Local luminaries such as dub poet Jean "Binta" Breeze appear alongside new writers – information can be found on Peter Howard's campoetry website. The Junction's Digital Disco events incorporate a new generation of poets into their musical mayhem. If you want to track down the next Sylvia Plath or Geoffrey Hill, grab a copy of the *May Anthologies* – yearly collections of the best student writing from Oxford and Cambridge, available from Waterstones and Heffers. While you're there, you might want to pick up *The Atlas of Literature* (edited by Malcolm Bradbury), which will be able to tell you where the original Sylvia Plath met husband Hughes – with a resounding slap, and, according to some sources, a bite on the cheek!

colleges

Much of the charm of central Cambridge stems from the intimate character of the college courts and the beauty of the ancient buildings. The most picturesque of the colleges are the oldest, mostly to be found along the river and around the city centre. These are all within a short walk of each other, mostly along the Backs, although some, such as Darwin College (above), are further along the river. Each college has its own distinctive character and unique history.

Colleges are generally headed by a Master or a Mistress, except for King's (a Provost), Queens', New Hall, Wolfson and Clare Hall (Presidents), Newnham (a Principal) and Robinson (a Warden). Other senior members of colleges are usually called Fellows. All are elected largely on the basis of their academic achievements. Most have heavy teaching and administrative duties, but all regard their research as equally important.

The number of students in each college varies from fewer than 100 to nearly 1000, of which usually two-thirds are undergraduates. Most colleges house all their undergraduates, and students may find themselves living in rooms that are centuries old. Whilst cheaper than city rents, collegiate rents have been the focus of great student dispute in recent years, as bursars have increased them to levels that many undergrads find unacceptable. Campaigns by CUSU, the students' union, and *Varsity*, the student newspaper, have highlighted rising unrest amongst the undergraduate and graduate student community, whilst rent strikes amongst college student unions have proliferated.

Visitors should bear in mind that the colleges are places where people live and work. For this reason, parts of many of the colleges remain closed altogether in the examination period in May and June. In addition, groups of ten or more people wishing to tour the colleges must be accompanied by a blue-badged Cambridge guide. Details are available from the Tourist Information Centre.

christ's

Where to find it: at the bottom of St. Andrew's Street, near Lion Yard and opposite the taxi rank.

Christ's was originally intended to be God's House, situated where King's now lies, but was displaced by Henry VI's plans to build his huge college.

Having moved to its current site in 1446, Christ's was not renamed and refounded until 1505 by Lady Margaret Beaufort (also the founder of St John's). The majority of students live in Sir Denys Lasdun's New Court, built in 1966: undergrads have aptly nicknamed it 'The Typewriter'.

Poet John Milton studied at Christ's, and was known as 'the lady of Christ's' by his fellow undergraduates. Charles Darwin, author of *The Origin of the Species*, is another of Christ's many famous alumnus. Within the University, Christ's has a deserved reputation for academic excellence, due to its frequent position at the top of the University league table that compares the examination results of each college. Non-Christ's students are often heard enviously attributing the success to the strict rules that forbid televisions in students' rooms and insist on the closure of the college bar at 8.30pm each evening.

churchill

Where to find it: a fair walk out of town, Churchill lies on Storey's Way, off Huntingdon Road.

Churchill is the national and Commonwealth monument that honours Sir Winston Churchill. It houses a selection of his papers in its Archive Centre, including a number of his personal writings, controversially bought and donated to the college with money from the National Lottery. Opened in the 1960s as an all-male college, Churchill became the first male college to admit women six years later.

Its buildings, on which construction began in 1960, are uncompromisingly of that era, with striking geometric construction. The gate to the porters' lodge, donated to the college by the British Aluminium Company, is itself a work of art, made of solid aluminium (cast to look like concrete) and designed to be openable by hand under the slightest pressure. The most recent buildings maintain this cutting-edge architectural theme.

The college was established to address the problem of Britain's shortage of scientists, and for this reason maintains a 70% intake of science, maths and engineering students.

clare

Where to find it: on Trinity Lane, behind Caius and the Senate House and overlooking the river.

Clare was founded in 1326 and looks onto the back of King's. This college didn't enjoy the most successful start, as lack of funds forced it to be re-founded by Lady Elizabeth de Clare only twelve years later. Few of the original buildings remain, due to a fire in the sixteenth century, so the buildings you can now see originate from the 1600s. Clare can boast the oldest bridge in Cambridge, decorated with stone balls. An old trick is to ask how many balls there are: the correct answer is thirteen and four-fifths, as one has had a segment shaved off.

The Fellows' Gardens are some of the prettiest open to the public and can provide somewhere peaceful to relax if the bustle of the town is becoming too tiring.

'Punt jousting' on the Backs behind Clare College

corpus christi

Where to find it: Trumpington Street, opposite Catz.

Uniquely amongst Cambridge colleges, Corpus was founded by the townspeople, by the guilds of Corpus Christi and the Blessed Virgin Mary, in 1352. Old Court, the oldest surviving Oxbridge courtyard, dates from soon after the foundation, while New Court was built in the 1820s by William Wilkins, who also designed Downing and much of King's. The Parker Library on the south side of New Court is home to one of Britain's greatest collections of medieval manuscripts. Bequeathed by the then Archbishop of Canterbury, and former Master of the College Matthew Parker in 1574, the collection includes the Canterbury gospels and the oldest known manuscript of the Anglo-Saxon chronicle.

Corpus is one of the smallest undergraduate colleges, but has a large number of graduate students, who are housed at the college's handsome Leckhampton site off Grange Road. Traditionally stronger in academic than in sporting life, Corpus' small size lends it a close atmosphere. The college's Fletcher Players run the highly successful Playroom theatre on St Edward's Passage, where much new student drama is performed. Famous old members include dramatist Christopher Marlowe, whose room can be seen in Old Court, Nobel Prize-winning physicist Sir George Paget Thompson, and disgraced former Tory MP Neil Hamilton.

downing

Where to find it: on Regent Street, along from Emma.

Due to legal wrangling between the family of its founder, Baronet Sir George Downing, and the University, the building of Downing was greatly delayed (and the legacy greatly reduced). Work started under William Wilkins in his neo-classical style during the early 19th century, but the college remained unfinished until modern times. Most recent additions include the Howard and Butterfield Buildings, and the Maitland Robinson Library, all built to Classical designs in the yellow-pink tinged Ketton stone that forms the earlier buildings. Downing's style differs from the other colleges; Wilkins moved away from the traditional courtyards to a lawned campus style which pre-dates that favoured by some American universities. Recognised within the University for its rowing prowess, Downing's Women's 1st Boat is often Head of the River, and thus hosts the ceremonial boat burning.

Downing was one of the last colleges to be established for general educational purposes according to the ancient tradition. Subsequently, most colleges have been founded to perform a particular educational need: for example, in Girton's case, to provide University education for women.

emmanuel

Where to find it: on St. Andrew's Street, opposite the Regal pub (a new addition to the Wetherspoon's chain, this is at time of writing the largest pub in Britain).

A little way along St. Andrew's Street is the 18th century entrance to Emmanuel (affectionately known as Emma). Another college founded on the site of an unfortunate Priory dissolved by Henry VIII, Sir Walter Mildmay (Queen Elizabeth I's Chancellor) created it in 1584 as 'a seed-plot of learned men'. He hoped it would provide priests for the newly established Protestant Church.

The original Priory buildings were adapted to reflect the changes in religious thinking: the old church was converted into a dining hall and the refectory into the Chapel. However, the new Chapel was never consecrated, and was replaced in 1677 by the current Chapel in First Court, designed by Sir Christopher Wren. Sir Walter's original aim was a success: many of the first Protestant settlers in New England were graduates of the college, including John Harvard, founder of Harvard University.

fitzwilliam

Where to find it: next to New Hall on Huntingdon Road (close to the Texaco Garage - a 24-hour shopping haven for hungry students).

Fitzwilliam, set up in 1869, existed for almost 100 years as Fitzwilliam House, for students who were unable to afford membership of any college. It was originally based on Trumpington Street, opposite the Fitzwilliam Museum. Fitz received its Charter to become a University college in 1966 when it moved to its current location from the former site at the other end of the town.

The buildings, mostly dating from the 1960s, are unrelentingly modern and of a dark brown brick: their modernity means that student rooms are relatively luxurious, all being equipped with telephone lines, and many with en suite showers. The college's spacious gardens are a further bonus to those who take the time to walk out to the Huntingdon Road site.

Famous ex-Fitz students include British politician and ex-Master of Emmanuel College, Lord St John of Fawsley, and the Singaporean leader Lee Kuan Yew.

girton

Where to find it: two and a half miles out from the city, Girton College is located on Huntingdon Road, further out than New Hall and Fitz.

Girton, established in 1869, was the first of the women's colleges. Originally located in the Hertfordshire town of Hitchin, in 1873 it moved to Girton Village, felt to be a safe distance from the male undergraduates of Cambridge. In 1979 the college admitted its first male undergraduates.

The college's picturesque neo-gothic architecture was in the main the creation of three generations of the Waterhouse family, the first of whom, Alfred Waterhouse, was responsible for the introduction of the corridor plan – rooms based around a corridor rather than a staircase as had previously been true of most college architecture.

gonville & caius

Where to find it: on Trinity Street, next to the Senate House.

One of the oldest, largest and richest colleges in Cambridge, Caius was founded, as Gonville Hall, by Edmund Gonville in 1348. After Henry VIII snatched much of the college's land for his new college, Trinity, Dr. Keys (who latinised his name to 'Caius', thus providing generations of freshers and visitors with cause for confusion) refounded it as Gonville and Caius in 1557.

Dr. Keys provided many of the delightful features the college is now known for, including the three gates to symbolise his ideal of a student's career. The Gate of Humility is now to be found in the Fellows' Garden, the Gate of Virtue provided the entrance to Caius Court, and the Gate of Honour (decorated with sundials and crests) leads to the Senate House. Caius students still walk through the Gate of Honour to the Senate House for their graduation ceremonies.

The greatest Caius legend is that of the Austin 7 – a black van hauled up to the roof of the Senate House by prankster students in June 1958.

homerton

Where to find it: on Hills Road, a fair bike ride out of town.

Homerton College is most well-known as the University of Cambridge's teacher training college, although it no longer offers solely teaching qualifications: its first BA degrees were presented in 1999.

The college relocated from Homerton Village in Middlesex to the outskirts of Cambridge in 1894. Shortly afterwards, in 1897, Homerton stopped admitting men, and only agreed to re-admit them as recently as 1978.

jesus

Where to find it: situated off Jesus Lane, the college is reached by a narrow walled passage.

Jesus' spacious grounds once belonged to the Priory of St Radegund in the early 12th century, before the Priory fell into disrepute and was refounded by a college. This was in 1496, thanks to John Alcock, the Bishop of Ely. The gatehouse stands at the end of a walled passage (nicknamed The Chimney), and through this First Court is found with the bronzed horse statue in the centre.

The Chapel, restored in the 19th century, contains ceiling designs by William Morris and some pre-Raphael stained glass. The college has several celebrated alumni including Prince Edward, Thomas Cranmer and the journalist Alastair Cook. Less celebrated at the time was the poet Samuel Taylor Coleridge, who was eventually sent down for bad behaviour and bad debts.

king's

Where to find it: at the centre of King's Parade, this college's renowned ornate structure is unmistakeable.

One of the most famous sights in Cambridge, William Wilkin's ornate gatehouse and King's Chapel stretch halfway along King's Parade, overshadowing their neighbours, the neo-classical Senate House and St Catharine's College. It was Henry VI's aim to build a huge college with an arcaded front court, bell tower and a cloistered court on the backs. Although the college was founded in 1441, and work started on the Chapel five years later, Henry VI's overthrow meant that most of the site remained empty for more than 300 years. This dismayed the locals who remembered the buildings that stood on the site before they were razed to make space for the college. It did take considerably less time to complete the Chapel, even though this task still took 69 years.

The Chapel draws huge numbers of visitors each year, including a film crew from the BBC each Christmas to film King's College Choir carol service, broadcast annually on Christmas morning. Sightseers are also attracted by Rubens' Adoration of the Magi, anonymously donated in 1972, which hangs behind the altar. Sadly, the most impressive and famous building in Cambridge is now in need of restoration where acid rain has begun to cause damage. In 1996, the college launched an appeal to try to raise the millions needed to carry out the work.

As well as its magnificent architecture, King's also attracts a lot of attention for the student protests staged there over the last decade, mainly concerning student poverty. Consequently, King's students have the reputation of being the most politically active in Cambridge.

magdalene

Where to find it: on Magdalene Street, situated next to Magdalene Bridge and overlooking the river.

Another example of confusing pronunciation that will catch out anyone who is not familiar with the city, Magdalene is pronounced 'maudlin'. The college is most famous for housing alumnus Samuel Pepys' 3000 volume library. The writer left the collection to his old college on his death in 1703. Still there, in its original red oak bookcases, the most highly prized treasure is Pepys' personal diary. Written in a secret code, it took three years to decipher.

The college was founded in 1428 as Buckingham college and originally only housed monks. This proved to be its downfall: before it was refounded in 1542 by Lord Audley of Walden, Magdalene had suffered huge losses as a result of Henry VIII's programme of dissolving the monasteries.

The Magdalene of today still has a reputation as a very traditional college; its annual May Ball is, unusually, white tie. Magdalene was also the last college to admit women, holding out until 1988, and only caving in as the college's academic results slipped compared to the results of other colleges which admitted both sexes.

new hall

Where to find it: on Huntingdon Road, beyond Fitzwilliam College.

Founded due to the success of a society that was formed with the sole aim of establishing a third Cambridge college for women. They succeeded in 1954, with the college originally starting out as a limited company situated near the Backs. New Hall later moved to its present site in 1964.

The most striking feature of the buildings (designed by Chamberlain, Powell and Bon) is the huge white dome over the dining hall (below), famous within the University ever since undergraduate pranksters painted big black footprints over it.

newnham

Where to find it: situated on Sidgewick Avenue, Newnham is directly opposite the Sidgewick Site, which houses the arts faculties.

The second college for women, Newnham was established in 1871 after Henry Sidgwick, a Trinity Fellow, rented houses to provide lodgings for female students. The college received its Charter in 1919, although it was not until 1948 that women were recognised as full members of the University.

Newnham does not have its own Chapel, being strictly non-denominational, but the college does boast the University's first building to have been designed by a woman. Elizabeth Whitworth Scott's Fawcett Building was named after Philippa Fawcett, who gained the highest marks in the University's maths examinations in 1890 but was refused a degree because of her gender.

pembroke

Where to find it: on Trumpington Street, just opposite Peterhouse.

This college can claim the first building to be completed by Sir Christopher Wren: the Pembroke chapel, on the site of the first college chapel to be built in Cambridge. Founded in 1347, the college has a particularly relaxed feel to it. The courts are open and seem more like gardens than the starkly manicured lawns that many colleges favour.

Found outside the library is a statue of William Pitt the Younger who became Prime Minister aged 25, only ten years after he began his studies at Pembroke. Other famous alumni include such diverse talents as Ted Hughes, Peter Cook and Eric Idle.

peterhouse

Where to find it: situated on Trumpington Street, Peterhouse lies between Little St. Mary's and the Fitzwilliam Museum.

Founded in 1284 by Hugh de Balsam, Bishop of Ely, Peterhouse predates all other colleges by over 100 years. Unfortunately, the only remaining building from this time is the Hall, where breath-taking examples of William Morris' stained glass and tiling can be found, although these date back only to its 1831 restoration.

From the front, the college appears much less imposing than many of its neighbours because of the slightly mixed-up layout. However, although home to only 200 students, the college's land stretches along the rear of Trumpington Street. Of the many students who have enjoyed their time here, the most famous include the poet Thomas Gray and the scientists Henry Cavendish and Charles Babbage.

queens'

Where to find it: on Silver Street, opposite the Anchor public house.

Originally founded as St. Bernard's college in 1446 by Queen Mary of Anjou (wife of Henry VII), the college was renamed and further work carried out on it by the wife of Henry VII's successor, Queen Elizabeth Woodville. Cloister Court is a beautiful Elizabethan courtyard dominated by the half-timbered President's lodge. The College is divided by the Cam, the two halves linked by the mathematical bridge. Many tour guides will tell you that this was built under the direction of Newton and originally did not need to be held together by nuts and bolts. This, however, is not true; Newton died 22 years before the bridge's construction.

robinson

Where to find it: on Grange Road, near the junction with Herschel Road, a few hundred yards out of town from Selwyn College.

The newest college. A gift of £18 million from its single benefactor, TV rental entrepreneur Sir David Robinson, ensured its establishment as the only Cambridge college founded with students of both sexes in mind. Opened by the Queen in 1981, the college occupies a twelve acre site near the University Library.

st. catharine's

Where to find it: between King's and Queens' colleges, near the corner of King's Parade and Silver Street.

Affectionately known as Catz by its students, St. Catharine's is located just opposite Corpus. The college was founded by King's provost in 1473 on land just to the South of its more famous neighbour. Most of the college dates from rebuilding completed in 1775. The front gate looks onto Trumpington Street and looking into the college from there the three closed sides of a typical, if uninspiring, courtyard can be seen. Previous students have included Dr John Addenbrooke (founder of the city's hospital) and William Wotton, who entered the college in 1675 aged nine and already fluent in Latin, Greek and Hebrew.

st. john's

St. John's Bridge of Sighs, seen at night

Where to find it: next to Trinity College, at the northern end of the town centre.

Rivalry between John's and its neighbour Trinity continues to this day. This is most apparent during the Bumps rowing races in the Lent and Easter terms. John's Boat Club was renamed Lady Margaret (after Lady Margaret Beaufort, the college's posthumous founder) at the turn of the century. It is rumoured that this followed an unfortunate incident when Trinity's cox was killed as their boat was bumped by John's, who had fixed a sharp spike to their stern. Now, every morning before the races, crews and supporters of each boat club congregate in their respective college for the 'stomp'. The two groups march through their own college before meeting on the Backs, where there is much jostling as each club attempts to capture the opposition's cox. Usually not much more than a college scarf is captured which is then hung from the top of the college boat house.

Founded in 1511, John's consists of a series of distinctively different courts. The First and Second Courts, in Tudor style, adjoin the 17th century Third Court. The gothic 19th century New Court is linked to the older parts of the College by Henry Hutchinson's Bridge of Sighs (opposite), an exquisite imitation of its namesake in Venice. Cripps, the newest building, is found behind New Court; it was completed in 1967. Despite looking somewhat out of place in its ancient setting, the building (which provides student accommodation) won awards for the innovation of its design.

selwyn

Where to find it: near Newnham on Grange Road.

Selwyn was founded in 1882 to make provision for those who intended to serve as missionaries abroad and to educate the sons of clergymen. Students were originally required to have been baptised as Christians, and fees were kept very low through public subscriptions to encourage poorer students.

sidney sussex

Where to find it: in the town centre, opposite the Sainsbury's supermarket.

A fairly small college in the city centre, the location of which has earned it the nickname 'Sidney Sainsbury's' among students. The Countess of Sussex, Lady Frances Sidney, bequeathed £5,000 to found the college on the site of a friary in 1596. The 16th and 17th century buildings were given their current appearance by Sir Jeffrey Wyattville in the early 19th century when he created the two uniform courts that front the college.

Despite its mundane nickname, this college probably boasts the most interesting legend of them all. Although Oliver Cromwell was a student at Sidney, the college supported the King in the English Civil War. After the Restoration, Charles II ordered Cromwell's body be exhumed and beheaded, but it was not until 1960 that it was re-buried. The head was given to the college and now rests in an unmarked location in Sidney's Chapel, buried amidst great secrecy with the Master, the Chaplain and three Fellows looking on.

Sidney Sussex was the last of the ancient colleges to be founded. It was not until 200 years later that any more colleges were established, the first of these being Downing in 1800.

trinity college

Where to find it: on Trinity Street

There are many things that Trinity is famous for: its size, its wealth, its alumni – all of which have given birth to many legendary stories.

It began with Trinity's famous founder, Henry VIII, who in 1547 ordered the amalgamation of two existing colleges (King's Hall and Michael House) to form the largest Cambridge college. Thomas Nevile worked on much of the college and created the Great Court, consisting of over two acres of lawn surrounding the fountain that once provided the whole college's water supply. Among the Tudor buildings is the clock tower, immortalised in the film Chariots of Fire, where a race was held around the outside of the court while the clock struck twelve. Eton was the actual location used in the film, but the race is re-created each year after a college feast – first year students attempt the Great Court Run, inevitably without success.

Behind the Great Court can be found Nevile's Court, which Nevile left open to the river that runs just behind it but which was closed off in 1695 by Sir Christopher Wren's library, now one of the city's most famous buildings. The library houses many original manuscripts, including works by Milton, Wittgenstein and AA Milne, amongst the limewood bookcases. From the outside it is not possible to judge the library's size, due to Wren's effort to conceal the height of floor level. Standing under the library, it is also possible to re-create Isaac Newton's experiment when he calculated the speed of sound. Just stamp your foot and listen for the thunder-clap echo.

Trinity is the biggest Oxbridge college, as well as the richest. Rumoured to be the third biggest landowner in the country, a popular myth is that you can walk all the way to Oxford on Trinity's land. More trustworthy facts about the college include that it has produced six British Prime Ministers and more Nobel Prize winners than the whole of France.

trinity hall

Where to find it: in the town centre next to Clare.

After the devastation caused by the plague, Bishop Bateman of Norwich founded Trinity Hall to train a new body of lawyers and priests. That was back in 1350 and since then Tit Hall (as it is colloquially known) has produced many eminent judges and lawyers. To this day it is still respected for its legal training. Unfortunately, Tit Hall is another college to have suffered fire damage and most of the 14th century main court had to be rebuilt or re-surfaced in 1852.

The novelist Henry James described the area around the old Elizabethan library as the prettiest corner of the world. It is also worth taking a quick look inside the library, where Jacobean bookcases contain the original texts that have been chained there for centuries to prevent theft. A new and very architecturally sympathetic library now looks out over Garret Hostel Bridge (background picture).

Tit Hall's Chapel may be the smallest in Cambridge but was completed in 1352 and now contains stained glass commemorating Robert Runcie, the college Dean between 1956 and 1960, who later became the Archbishop of Canterbury.

the remaining six colleges

Cambridge University also comprises six other colleges. Most of the were founded over the last two centuries for graduate students or mature undergraduates. Hughes Hall, Darwin (below), St Edmund's (most famous for being the college where many of Cambridge Blues rowers study), Wolfson and Clare Hall are all mainly for graduate students. Lucy Cavendish is unique in Europe as the only college specifically for mature women who wish to resume their studies in any discipline.

university life

a year in cambridge

michaelmas term

October: The Cambridge academic year commences at the beginning of October – later than at most other universities – and each of the three terms last only eight weeks, considerably shorter than everywhere else (except Oxford). This would lead some to believe that Cambridge students have it easy and do less work than other students, but this is not the case. The University's unofficial motto is 'work hard, play hard' and you have to with all your work, sport and socialising crammed into such a short time.

Term starts with Freshers' Week. This is the week when all the new students arrive and are introduced to Cambridge life before lectures begin. Each college's student union will organise its own activities for the first years, usually including drinks parties, meals and pub crawls. Many colleges also assign each fresher college 'parents': two second or third year students who can show their 'children' around.

One place all freshers go during this week is to the local sports hall where the Societies Fair is held. Inside the bustling hall, members of every University society stand at stalls recruiting members for the new year, offering incentives ranging from the ever popular free drinks to flying lessons. There are hundreds of societies to choose between, from the cultural and the charitable to sports and silliness.

Further into term, Matriculation Dinner is held by all the colleges. This is a formal college feast where new students are ceremoniously welcomed into their college by its fellows. The meal often consists of at least four courses and everyone is expected to wear academic dress (gowns). This is often followed by much less formal drinks parties held by Tutors for their new students.

November: With lectures and supervisions well under way, November offers the chance to settle down and train for all the sports you were persuaded to take up during Freshers' Week. Nearly everyone at Cambridge tries rowing for the college at some stage – most often in the first term. Rowing is taken very seriously, with some colleges having five or more men's boats (with eight rowers and a cox in each boat) and at least three women's boats, all of whom train at least four times per week. This term is viewed as a training term to coach all the new rowers and spot talent for the higher boats. This culminates in Fairburns, a race at the end of term which novice boats can enter.

Also during this time, many intercollegiate sports tournaments, 'Cuppers', begin. This often means two matches each weekend for hockey, football or rugby players.

December: The Michaelmas term ends early in December, and this is marked by many colleges with a Christmas dinner, as well as the traditional pantomime staged by Cambridge's two foremost dramatic societies, the ADC and Footlights. Adapted from traditional stories, the pantomimes are permanently sold out, always very funny and never suitable for young children! The pantomime has been held at the ADC theatre for decades: many of Britain's most famous comedians (for example, Emma Thompson, Stephen Fry and John Cleese) started their careers there.

Another Cambridge institution is King's College Chapel Choir, which is filmed each year by the BBC, singing carols in the famous Chapel, to be broadcast on Christmas morning.

The beginning of December is also interview time, so, as the current students leave, hopeful candidates arrive to compete for places (dependent on school exam results) at Cambridge the following year.

The last big Cambridge event before Christmas is the annual Varsity rugby match held against Oxford. The match, played at Twickenham, is televised around the world and the cameras often show crowds of student supporters with faces painted in traditional university colours, Cambridge's light blue and Oxford's dark blue. Many of the players seen here go on to compete internationally – it was only a few years ago that the Cambridge side contained Gavin Hastings and Rob Andrews, who went on to captain England and Scotland respectively.

lent term

January: Cambridge looks very pretty in the snow, but when the students return from the Christmas break it is bitterly cold, with harsh winds blowing across the flat fens. Now is the time when many decide that getting up at 6am to get to the boat house at first light is torture, and the boat clubs lose quite a few members.

In January, elections are held, both to choose the new members of the college student unions, and to elect the officers of the Cambridge University Student Union. At college level, the agendas of some candidates are often based more on the opening hours of the college bar and the drinks it serves than on the more serious issues dealt with by CUSU.

The fund-raising work of Cambridge Rag starts now. In order to raise money for charity, students get involved in Rag-organised fun events such as Rag Blind Date and Rag Assassins. The latter involves being assigned a target (another student), with the aim of shooting them with a water pistol. A prize eventually goes to the assassin who 'kills' the most of his or her fellow students.

February: The Rag activities culminate this month with the annual hitch to Europe. All the fancy-dressed hitchers meet up in a European city and have to raise as much money as possible on their way there.

In the fourth week of this term, the second college feasts of the year are held. Halfway Dinner is not as formal as either Matriculation dinner or Graduation Dinner, but is held as a celebration for second years halfway through their courses who cannot go to either of the other feasts that year.

March: The highlight of the term for those rowers who lasted through the winter is the Lent Bumps. This is one of the two major collegiate rowing races of the year (the other being the May Bumps). All college boats have places in one of eight divisions, and for four days all seventeen boats will line up a length and a half apart according to their positions in the division. They race to catch up with the boat ahead, beginning as the starting gun is fired. This often leads to confusion and sometimes accidents and chaos as boats attempt to hit each other. A bump is scored if a college's boat catches the boat ahead of them before the boat chasing them hits their boat. If this is completed successfully, the boat moves up a place for the following day. In the higher divisions, where all the crews are very fast, there is often not much bumping. However, in the lower divisions, results can be spectacular, as the differences between crews can be great, resulting in boats actually overtaking the boat they were chasing and bumping the boat ahead of them. This is an over-bump and the crew moves up two places.

In the evening of the last day of races each college will celebrate its success with a Boat Club

Dinner. Special celebrations will be held in those colleges of the Clubs that are top of the Men's first and Women's first divisions at the end of the competition. These colleges celebrate being Head of the River by burning a wooden boat in the grounds. It is also traditional for the triumphant crew to jump over the boat as it blazes.

A safer activity has to be going to see the Marlowe Society's annual production at the Arts Theatre. The show is usually professionally directed and designed, starring the best of the University's acting talent, and is often an unusual verse play (Caryl Churchill's Serious Money and Orson Welles' Moby Dick Rehearsed are recent productions.)

April: Rowing remains the focus well into the Easter vacation as the build up to the Boat Race starts. Although college rowers are now spectators rather than participators, the event is a very important one in students' diaries, as they congregate (often in pubs) along the course of the race between Putney and Mortlake on the Thames.

The boat race is always a hotly contested national event that Cambridge crews have won convincingly many times in the past decade. A particular triumph was in 1993, when Cambridge beat a semi-professional Oxford crew captained by Olympic gold medallist, Matthew Pinsent.

easter term

May: A very quiet month, due to the exams held at the end. Most people work hard, and hectic social lives are temporarily put on hold as studies become tense. (It is also worth noting that many colleges close their doors to visitors during this period.) However, the end of exams is celebrated in spectacular fashion.

June: The first Sunday after all the exams are over (known as Suicide Sunday) is a day for garden parties and relaxation. Societies at different colleges hold parties in the Fellows' Gardens serving punch and fresh strawberries to their guests, who relax in the sun and listen to the jazz bands organised by their hosts.

This Sunday also heralds the beginning of May Week, celebrations which were originally held in May: the name has stuck despite the change of date. This is the week when all the May Balls are held to end the year in the traditional style.

Just before May Week, college rowers have their final opportunity for sporting glory in the May Bumps (or 'Mays'). This is exactly the same in format as the Lent Bumps, although it is always regarded as the more important event, and is certainly the one favoured by spectators who are happy to gather at the pubs along the river to watch. This, like the Lent Bumps, culminates in a college being crowned Head of the River, and is celebrated by the traditional boat burning.

Famous for their extravagance, luxury and expense, May Balls are still regarded by most of the University's students as the high point of the year. The events take place in the grounds of the colleges and much preparation goes into the decorations, with lighting and flowers used to create a fairy tale atmosphere. Many Balls are themed; in recent years there have been 'Midsummer Night's Dream', 'Murder Mystery' and 'Firecracker'.

All, however, contain the essential ingredients: champagne, fireworks and a number of bands to entertain the students in their lavish ball gowns or smart dinner jackets as they dance away the night. Most exam results are announced just after May Week and it is common to see crowds of students surrounding the screens outside the Senate House, trying to see what their year's work amounted to. Grades at British universities are divided into four classes: first, upper second, lower second, and third. Most students are happy with either of the first two.

At the end of June, the Senate House again becomes crowded as the setting for the graduation ceremonies. Graduands (those who are about to graduate) dress up in full academic robes – white bow ties, gowns and an 'ermine' hood. At the ceremony, those receiving their degrees have to hold one of the Vice-Chancellor's fingers in groups of four, while he gives a Latin declaration.

This officially marks the end of the academic year, and for students returning for the next academic year, it's off on the 'long vacation' until October.

a day in the life of the university

There is no typical day in the life of a Cambridge student. Whilst a diligent science student may spend all day in lecture hall and library, a history student passionate about theatre may be spending all day and all night preparing for his or her production, putting off an essay to the last possible minute. Hence, the following outline highlights some elements that may occur in a day at some stage of the academic year, and range from the mundane to the magical.

5.30am Hardened and dedicated (or mad) boat crews descend on the river Cam to get their all important practice at one of those rare times when all Cambridge is calm – except the boathouses.

7.30am Some students get some early morning exercise at the swimming pool to prepare them for the rigours of the day ahead, whilst others frantically finish off essays for an impending supervision.

8am Breakfast, either in students' rooms or in the more luxuriant setting of their College's Hall. The room-cleaners (bedders) start their daily duty of helping keep things tidy, and those intending to get up later may be awoken by their bedder knocking on their door. Bedders have the right (and the keys) to enter students' rooms every morning except Sunday, and the traditional 'do not disturb' sign is to put one's waste bin outside the door. Bins outside doors are, naturally, the source of much gossip amongst neighbours, who may jump to conclusions as to just why someone does not wish to be disturbed.

9am Lectures begin, and typically last one hour. The number of lectures a student is expected to attend is determined by the subject they study. Science students tend to have significantly more lectures than arts students, and the latter often decide to be more selective about those lectures they grace with their presence. Others may go to their college or Faculty libraries to work in peace and quiet. On Fridays, Varsity, the student newspaper, arrives with the Porters, so there is often a mad rush to pick up this journalistic masterpiece!

1pm Lunch in Hall will be well underway, and the roads and colleges tend to be busy with students coming from lectures to get something to eat to prepare them for the afternoon's activities.

2pm Often students have supervisions in the afternoons, which help them explore their understanding of a specific topic in a way unique to Oxbridge. Many students will take the opportunity for some relaxation in the afternoon, often by playing a sport. This may be for a College or even University team, or just for fun. In the Summer, the tennis courts are always a popular venue, but throughout the year there are a huge number of sporting opportunities available to students. Others may prepare to enjoy the sun on the backs, or relax with a game of pool.

3pm In the Summer, after the stress of exams, there are numerous Garden Parties thrown by societies, which offer entertainments and drinks. They are always popular and invariably enjoyable. There will also be a variety of student plays, performed in college gardens, to go watch to while away the afternoon.

5.45-7pm Dinner will be served in Hall. Many students tend to eat in Hall at some stage during the day since it is convenient and fairly cheap. However, this may well depend on that day's menu!

7.30pm Formal Hall starts. This experience is unique to Oxbridge, and was traditionally the smart dinner of the evening. It is a three-course affair, with waiter service by candlelight. Hence, it is more expensive than the ordinary cafeteria dinner, and is often attended by students celebrating an occasion, for instance a birthday. Most colleges like students to dress smartly, often in a suit, and some insist that gowns be worn.

8pm Student plays start at the ADC Theatre in Park Street, the oldest university playhouse in Britain. The ADC is the centre of Cambridge's distinguished drama scene, but there are many other venues including the Playroom on St. Edward's Passage and college theatres such as Queens' Fitzpatrick Hall. Student productions are usually plentiful and of a high quality, and on occasion the plays are written by the students themselves. Several Cambridge drama groups annually put on shows at the Edinburgh Fringe Festival, and the University has produced its fair share of actors/actresses and directors over the years. Also at this time, a concert may begin at the University's West Road concert hall, or one of the many College Choirs may give an impressive recital.

8.15pm Other University societies will have a vast range of events to attend throughout the week. Some, like the Cambridge Forum, may hold debates with famous speakers, whilst others may get together for more bizarre reasons, reflecting the diversity of societies in which students may participate. Students blessed without two left feet may attend a class with the extremely popular Cambridge Dancers Club, which offers lessons helping with a variety of styles and types of dance. Other students may relax by listening to one of the many student radio shows that offer entertainment throughout the day.

9pm On a Friday or Saturday night there will be a variety of Ents to attend. These will include college discos (known as 'bops'), though they tend only to fill up much later. They are always well-attended – partly since they offer a variety of cheap and interesting drinks – and there are some extremely good regular events throughout the year catering for all tastes, from general 'cheese' to more specific genres.

10pm On the weekend, undergraduate parties will begin around this time. These are often to celebrate birthdays, and may be themed... for instance James Bond, or Austin Powers. Permission has to be sought from the Senior Tutor for these boisterous occasions, and porters often enjoy keeping a close eye on such events and terminating them when they feel necessary.

10.15pm College bars tend to fill up around this time. Most students can be sure of seeing their friends either here or in the JCR (common room) at night. The size and quality of college bars varies greatly. Other students may go outside the college to local pubs, whilst others may start to venture to one of the several nightclubs in Cambridge, the most popular appearing to be Fifth Avenue (affectionately known as Cindy's).

11pm Lateshows start at the ADC and Playroom theatres. Footlights traditionally holds its bi-termly 'smokers' at this time in the ADC. These are comedy revues where the most talented comics in Cambridge exercise their considerable talents to the appreciation of theatre audiences. Others may attend a late-night film at the Warner Village cinema in the Grafton centre.

12am At some stage during their time at Cambridge, most students will indulge in the experience that is Midnight Punting. Often an eye-opening way to spend the early hours of the morning!

2am Those parties that have not already been stopped by the porters tend to peter out around this time, and people find their way back to bed. Some colleges maintain a system where 'late keys' must be signed out of the porters' lodge to gain re-admission after a certain time, in order to keep tabs on the students.

3am Some students may still be awake in order to finish off an essay at the last minute, or simply to decrease the mountain of work piled up on their desks. Most students have the misfortune of an 'essay crisis' at some time, which turns into 'The Fear' during exams!

5am In May Week, this is when the 'survivors' photo' will be taken at the close of a May Ball, so that students have permanent evidence of an already extremely memorable night of decadence and fun.

cambridge dictionary

A long way: Anywhere more than five minutes' walk away.
Backs, n: The area between the backs of the colleges and Queens' Road, close to the Cam.
Bedder, n: Member of college staff (now always female) who makes students' beds and cleans their rooms.
Boatie, n: Rower, usually with same characteristics as a Rugger-bugger, qv.
Bop, n: disco, sometimes with food, always with drink.
Bumps, n: Complicated rowing races in which each college boat tries to catch up with the next.
'Cambridge' (as in 'so Cambridge'), adj: Used to describe something that is meant to characterise student life, usually with sense of somebody taking something to extremes.
Cambridge Student, The, n: Student rag purporting to compete with Varsity, qv.
Cindy's n: Reference to Fifth Avenue, nightclub, usually derogatory.
Compsci, n: Student reading computer science, usually derogatory. See Natsci, qv.
Confie, n: Conference delegate (usually used in combination with irritation about 'how delegates take over colleges outside term'.)
Death Van, n: Immensely popular late night fast-food stall.
Desmond (also Dezzy), n: Lower second in exams, usually finals. From Desmond Tutu (two-two).
Easter, n: Third term in the Cambridge academic year.
Emma, n: Emmanuel College
Entz, n (pl): Entertainments (usually provided by college JCRs).
Fitz, n: 1. Fitzwilliam College.
2. The ~ The Fitzwilliam Museum
Gardies, n: The Gardenia late-night takeaway in Rose Crescent.
Grantchester, n: Haven of peace and tranquility away from the hubbub of town (if you can get there, see Punt, qv)
Gyp room, n: Small kitchen for student use, habitually with a few gas rings and no oven (from gyp, obsolete term for male bedder).
Hack, n: Excessively motivated, often selfish, student who attempts to get to the top of undergraduate politics or journalism.
JCR, n: Junior Combination Room. Either an undergraduate common room, or the students elected to look after undergraduate affairs by their peers.
King's Street Run, n: Tour of the King's St pubs, in each of which the participants must drink a pint.
Lent, n: Second term of the Cambridge academic year.
Mathmo, n: Student reading Mathematics.
May Week, n: Week in June (confusingly) when May Balls occur (f. original month when balls were held).
Michaelmas, n: First term of the Cambridge academic year
Natsci, n: Student of natural sciences, usually derogatory.
Pidge or P/hole, n: Student's mail pigeon-hole (abbrev.)
Playroom, n, 1: Studio theatre off St. Edwards Passage. 2: Senior Combination Room.
Plodge, n: Porters' Lodge (abbrev.)
Porter, n: Member of college staff responsible for maintaining order and assisting visitors.
Pimms, n: Tipple of choice at May Week garden parties.
Punt, n: Instrument of social torture for the inexperienced user.
Rag, n: students' fund-raising charity. Also ~ Week. (f. obs. Rag=jape)
Rugger-bugger, n: Rugby-player, esp. one given to rowdy behaviour and drunkenness.
Shark, v.t.: To pursue members of the opposite sex unscrupulously.
Squash, n: Open meeting at start of year (usually with alcohol provided) of a college or University society for the purposes of recruiting new members.
Thesp, 1, n: Student actor or actress, usually with associated pretentiousness and tendency to show off. 2. v.i. To act. 3. v.i. To behave in a thespy (adj) manner.
Tit Hall, n: Trinity Hall, a college in its own right, not part of Trinity (abbrev.)
Vac, n: Vacation. (abbrev.)
Varsity, n: Immensely professional student newspaper published every Friday of term.

map of central cambridge

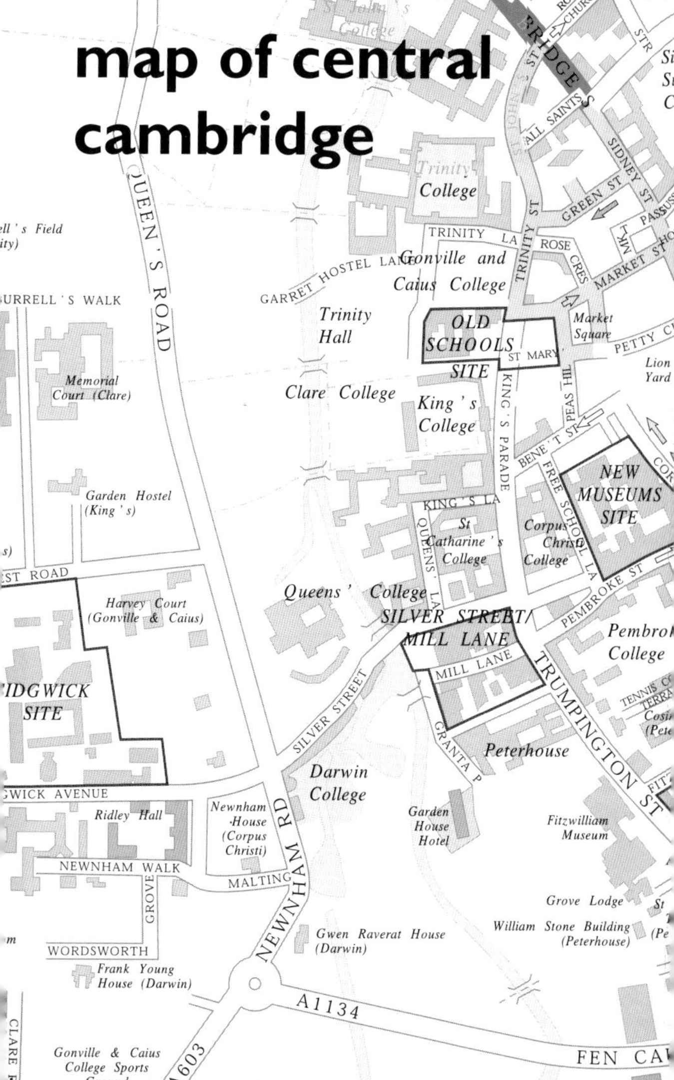

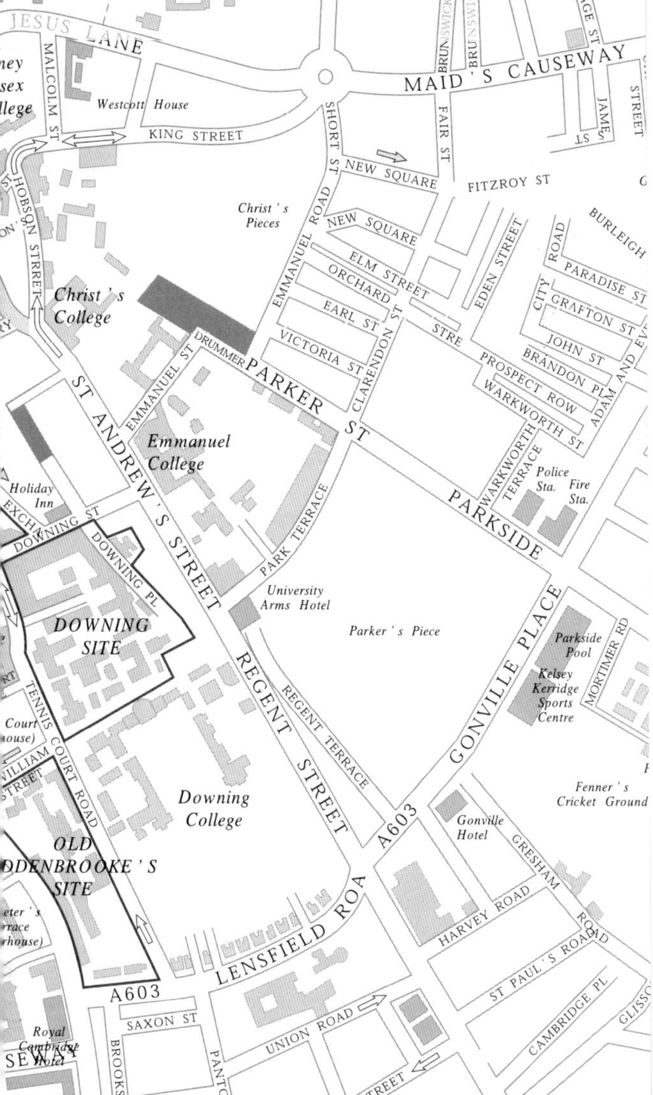
JESUS LANE
MALCOLM ST
Westcott House
KING STREET
HOBSON STREET
Christ's College
Christ's Pieces
MAID'S CAUSEWAY
BRUNSWICK
SHORT ST
FAIR ST
NEW SQUARE
FITZROY ST
JAMES ST
EMMANUEL ROAD
ELM STREET
ORCHARD ST
EARL ST
VICTORIA ST
CLARENDON ST
EDEN STREET
BURLEIGH
PARADISE ST
CITY ROAD
GRAFTON ST
JOHN ST
BRANDON PL
PROSPECT ROW
WARKWORTH ST
WARKWORTH TERRACE
ADAM AND EVE
DRUMMER
PARKER ST
EMMANUEL ST
Emmanuel College
ST ANDREW'S STREET
Holiday Inn
DOWNING ST
DOWNING PL
DOWNING SITE
PARK TERRACE
Police Sta.
Fire Sta.
PARKSIDE
University Arms Hotel
Parker's Piece
GONVILLE PLACE
Parkside Pool
Kelsey Kerridge Sports Centre
MORTIMER RD
REGENT STREET
REGENT TERRACE
TENNIS COURT ROAD
Downing College
Fenner's Cricket Ground
A603
Gonville Hotel
GRESHAM ROAD
OLD ADDENBROOKE'S SITE
LENSFIELD ROAD
HARVEY ROAD
ST PAUL'S ROAD
CAMBRIDGE PL
UNION ROAD
SAXON ST
Royal Cambridge Hotel
STREET

walk five: modern architecture

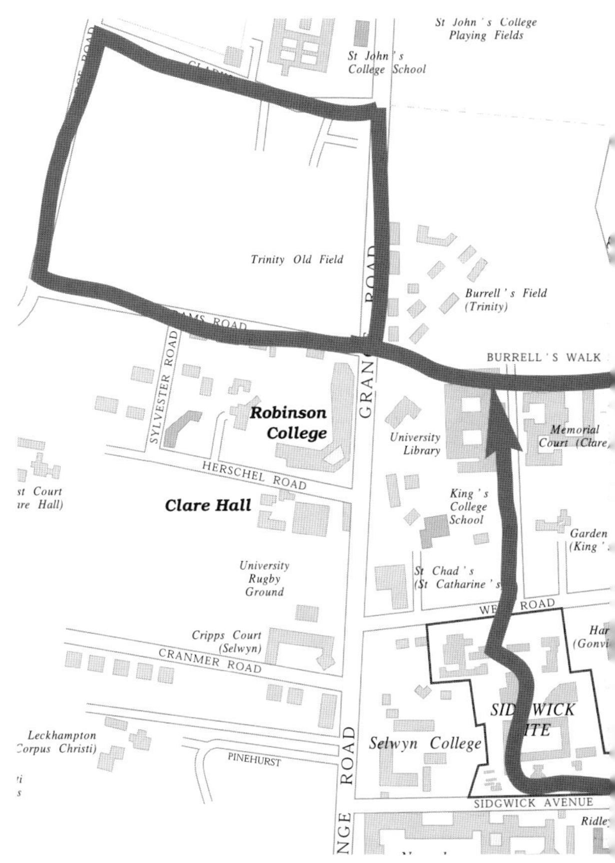

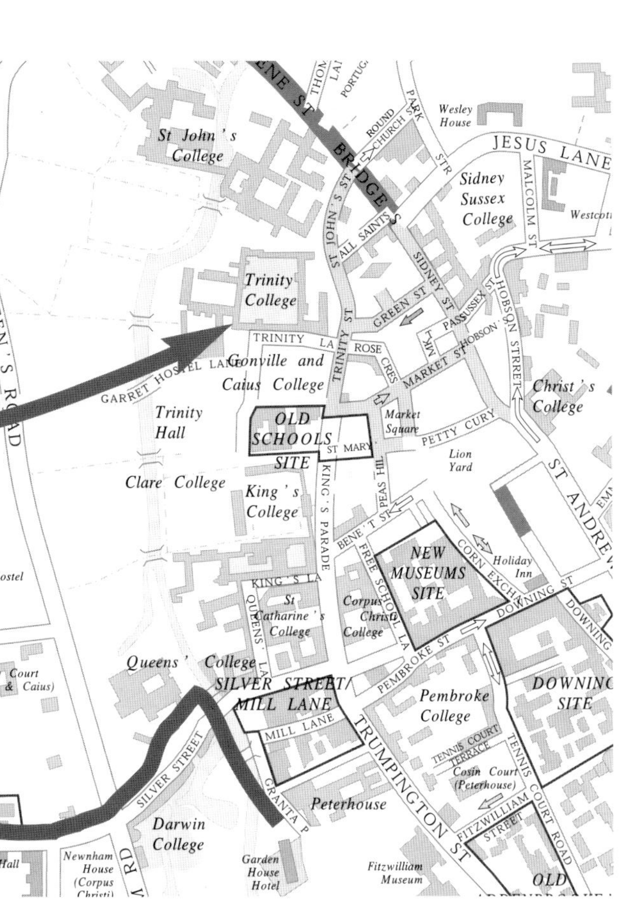

St John's College
BRIDGE ST
ROUND CHURCH ST
PARK ST
Wesley House
JESUS LANE
Sidney Sussex College
MALCOLM ST
ST JOHN'S ST
ALL SAINTS
SIDNEY ST
Trinity College
GREEN ST
SUSSEX ST
HOBSON STREET
TRINITY LA
TRINITY ST
ROSE CRES
MKT PASS
HOBSON'S
MARKET ST
GARRET HOSTEL LANE
Gonville and Caius College
Christ's College
Trinity Hall
OLD SCHOOLS SITE
ST MARY'S
Market Square
PETTY CURY
Lion Yard
ST ANDREW'S
Clare College
King's College
KING'S PARADE
PEAS HILL
BENE'T ST
NEW MUSEUMS SITE
CORN EXCHANGE
Holiday Inn
FREE SCHOOL LA
KING'S LA
St Catharine's College
Corpus Christi College
QUEENS' LA
DOWNING ST
DOWNING
Queens' College
PEMBROKE ST
SILVER STREET/MILL LANE
MILL LANE
Pembroke College
DOWNING SITE
TRUMPINGTON ST
TENNIS COURT TERRACE
TENNIS COURT ROAD
Cosin Court (Peterhouse)
SILVER STREET
GRANTA P
Peterhouse
FITZWILLIAM STREET
Darwin College
Newnham House (Corpus Christi)
Garden House Hotel
Fitzwilliam Museum
OLD
Hostel
Hall

walks and tours

walk one: the riverside colleges

Facing King's College Porters' Lodge, turn right along King's Parade. Just after King's College Chapel on your left, you will see a large neo-classical building, the Senate House, and opposite it on the right, Great St. Mary's Church.

A large University assembly hall, the Senate House fulfils a number of functions, most importantly as an examination hall and as the place where degrees are given out at the end of a student's time at Cambridge. The boards outside the Senate House are covered with sheets of examination results towards the end of the Easter Term (from the end of May and throughout June).

The Senate House was the scene of the most famous undergraduate joke derived from the sport of 'night-climbing' amidst the rooves of Cambridge. In June of 1958, students from Gonville and Caius

College (p.28), situated next door to the Senate House, achieved the near-impossible night-time feat of winching an old Austin van to the summit of the Senate House roof unspotted. The city awoke to consternation. A more recent attempt at a similar stunt involved scaling King's Chapel one night and fixing a banner 38 feet long reading 'Peace in Vietnam' between the towers facing King's Parade. The climbers responsible, however, were caught by police after climbing onto the Senate House roof, and 'sent down' (expelled) from the University.

Go through the traffic barriers into a cobbled area, with Senate House on your left. In front of you is Gonville and Caius College (always shortened simply to 'Caius', the name is pronounced 'keys' as it is the latinised name of the college's co-founder, Dr John Keys). Veer to the left and turn down a small cobbled alley, Senate House Passage, keeping the Senate House on your left. Follow this alley to the end.

As you pass down the alley, notice the elaborate gate on your right. This is Cauis' Gate of Honour, crowned by sundials, and made to an Italian model. It is the third of three gates which Dr John Keys deigned for Caius' students to pass through during their time at the college. The others were the Gates of Humility and Virtue.

At the end of Senate Passage, you will notice an alley to the left. If you follow down here, you will arrive at Clare College (p.22) on your right, and the visitors' entrance to King's College Chapel.

If you wish to continue on the route of this walk, however, turn right at the end of Senate House Passage, passing the entrance to Trinity Hall (p.46) on the left. Shortly afterwards, turn left again down Garret Hostel Lane. There should be the legend 'To the River' marked in chalk on one of the walls of this lane, with an arrow pointing down it.

Follow this lane over the steep pedestrianised Garret Hostel Bridge. Standing on the bridge and looking back the way you have come, you will see the newest addition to Trinity Hall, the modern and striking Jerwood Library, built to complement the ancient architecture which surrounds it (Trinity Hall dates from 1350).

Once over the bridge, you will notice that the path continues until it meets a main road (Queens' Road); off this path, there are two parallel paths off to the left. Take the first of these paths, keeping to trees and the road to your right. You are now on Cambridge's famous Backs (you can see the backs of the riverside colleges from this area). Carry on along the Backs until you see the spleandour of King's College over a field to your left. If you see people seemingly floating along in front of the lawns next to the chapel, don't worry, you're not hallucinating – they are punting. The path will end in a line of barriers just after you see King's Chapel, and you will notice a gateway to the back of the college on your left. The path has led you onto the pavement beside Queens' Road.

On the gate through to King's, there are two small crests, one with three roses in the lower half of the shield and another with three fleur de lys. The rose-covered crest is that of King's; the crest to the right of it, featuring lilies, is that of Eton College, the famous English Public School. King's and Eton were founded to complement one another – Eton scholars were intended to continue their education at this college.

Go through or around the barriers and take the footpath which crosses the green space diagonally to your left. (If this presents difficulties for wheelchairs, follow Queens' Road and take the first left turning down Silver Street, where this short cut ends). At the end of the path, turn left onto Silver Street.

Follow Silver Street over the Cam. As you pass over the bridge, look to your left and you will see Queens' College and its famous Mathematical Bridge. The multifarious legends surrounding this bridge include the suggestion that the bridge was originally built to a mathematical design that would allow it to stand with no bolts or nails holding it together.

Shortly after you have crossed the river, you will see Queens' Lane off to your left, which leads to the visitors' entrance to Queens' College. If you are not visiting Queens', carry on up Silver Street until it turns sharply to the right into Trumpington Street, next to Ede and Ravenscroft, the gentleman's outfitters' shop on the corner.

At this junction, turn left into Trumpington Street. You will pass St. Catharine's College on your left, and Corpus Christi College on your right. Follow this road until you see King's Porters' Lodge on your left.

walk two: the central colleges

Facing King's College Porter's Lodge, turn left along King's Parade. Carry on straight ahead as it turns into Trumpington Street opposite No. 1 King's Parade Restaurant. You will pass Corpus Christi College on your left and St. Catharine's College on your right. Soon, you will reach a junction, with St. Bene't's church on your left.

At the junction, carry on along the left side of Trumpington Street for a few metres, until you see St. Botolph's Lane off to the left. Follow this small road to its end. Next, veer right and you will reach Pembroke Street. Turn left, and follow this road right to its end at a T-junction and traffic lights. You will find that its name changes to Downing Street after 20 metres or so.

When you reach the end of this road, you will see a large classical entrance over the road in front of you. This is Emmanuel College, famous for its former student John Harvard, founder of the Massachusetts university, and, amongst contemporary University students, for its ducks. Turn left at the T-junction into St. Andrew's Street. When the road bends around to the right, carry on straight ahead over the cobbles, following St. Andrew's Street. After a while, the road will fork, and you will see an ornate gatehouse on the right. This is the entrance to Christ's College (p 20). Take the left-hand fork.

You will notice that you are either passing through or going around a set of gates. These, and the various other traffic obstacles that you will see at certain junctions around the city, are part of Cambridge City Council's controversial scheme which bans bicycles and traffic from the centre of town. Most spectacular are the obstacles which rise from and descend into the road to allow particular vehicles access to the restricted area. Follow Sidney Street as it bends slightly to the right. When Market Street joins from the left just after the branch of Woolworth's, carry on straight ahead along Sidney Street. About 40 metres or so along this road you will see a college gate to your right and Sainsbury's supermarket opposite, on your left.

The college on your right is Sidney Sussex College (above), sometimes known to students as 'Sidney Sainsbury's', because of its proximity to the supermarket. Perhaps fed-up with this nickname, students from the college once painted a pedestrian crossing across Sidney Street from the entrance of their college to the entrance of Sainsbury's, and proceeded to use it until it was removed.

When Sidney Street reaches a junction go straight on into Bridge Street ahead of you. After 40 metres or so, you will see church on your right. This is the Round Church (the origin of its name is self-evident).

To the right of the Round Church as you face it you will see a small alleyway, and a notice which shows the way to the Cambridge Union Society. One of the largest and oldest student societies (it was founded in 1815), it provides a forum for political and social debate. 'The Union', as it is known, still attracts many politicians and personalities to speak at its weekly debates.

The tradition of Union politics is so strong that it has been suggested that there is something of a 'Cambridge Mafia' in the British Conservative Party today. Carry on a little way along Bridge Street until St. John's Street branches off to your left. Turn into St. John's Street. On your right, you will notice the immense edifice of St. John's College Chapel, and, further along, the entrance to the college (p.41). Carry on along St. John's Street and you will come to Trinity College Great Gate (see right), again on your right.

If you look up at the statue of Henry VIII, founder of the college, in the centre of the gate, you will notice that he is not holding a sceptre in his right hand, but a chair-leg. This is testimony to the dangerous undergraduate sport of night-climbing, the scaling of university buildings under the cover of darkness. Some time in the early nineteenth century, when it was the fashion for fellows to wear wigs, the barber serving Trinity was bribed by undergraduates to climb up the college library and put the best wigs belonging to the Senior Fellows on the heads of the statues facing the Hall.

Continue along the same street, which has now become Trinity Street. You will pass Heffers, the city's most encyclopaedic bookshop, on your left, and some way further along, Gonville and Caius (pronounced 'keys') College on your right (above, pictured with the Senate House, and p.28). Carry on along Trinity Street until you see King's College Chapel over to the right as you reach the junction with St. Mary's Street. Cross over the road, through the barriers, and head up King's Parade, remaining on the left side of the road.

Carry on along King's Parade, and you will find yourself at King's College Porter's Lodge once more.

walk three: grantchester meadows

Grantchester, with its winding streets and thatched roofs, has long been a retreat for students. Just far enough out of Cambridge to feel 'away', undergraduates take to the village for a quiet drink in one of the pubs, as a destination for a long punting trip, or purely to see some countryside. The village's name is derived from the Cam's other name, the 'Granta'. The poet Rupert Brooke nostalgically recalled the two years (1910-1912) he spent in the 17th-century Old Vicarage in his well-known poem Grantchester, and the house is now home to the popular novelist Jeffrey Archer.

The Orchard Tea Gardens is an excellent place to stop and rest once you have reached Grantchester. Wittgenstein, Virginia Woolf and John Maynard Keynes have taken tea amongst the trees here, and its bohemian atmosphere and comfortable deck-chairs are ideal for relaxation on a fine summer's day (inside seating is available when the weather is unkind). In the summer, undergradute plays are often presented here.

If you are in search of stronger refreshment, Grantchester boasts three good pubs; The Green Man,

The Red Lion, and The Rupert Brooke, all of which also serve food. The best views are available from The Rupert Brooke. All three pubs are on the route of the walk below. This walk takes the visitor to the village the classic way, through Grantchester Meadows beside the Cam. Facing King's Porter's Lodge, turn left and follow King's Parade and Trumpington Street to the junction with Silver Street, just by St. Botolph's church. On your way, you will pass St. Catharine's College on your right and Corpus Christi College on your left.

Keep going straight ahead over the junction, crossing onto the right side of the road, where you will see a large Gothic building. This is the old site of the Cambridge University Press, now the Pitt Building. Walking to the far end of this building you will come to Mill Lane on your right. Follow Mill Lane past the University Careers Service and the Department of Pure Maths until you reach the Mill Pub, a favourite with students in the summer when they have finished their exams.

Opposite the pub you will see a gate and bridge over the Cam. Cross the river and follow the path beside it, which veers to the left. When the path forks, take the right-hand path. Walk across two bridges, reaching a junction of paths. Take the left-hand path alongside a stream on the right. Cross the main road and continue across the green, named Lammas Land, on the path in front of you until you come to another main road. Turn left along this road and carry on straight ahead into Granchester Street close by.

Grantchester Meadows

Follow Granchester Street until you reach the third road on the right, Eltisley Avenue. Go to the end, then take the road straight in front of you which veers slightly to the right. Carry on into a gravelled car park, following the Public Footpath sign to Granchester. At the end of the car park, take a narrow hedged byway which leads to Granchester Meadows through a gate. Follow the long tarmac path through the meadows through three more gates.

Carry on straight ahead through another gate until you reach a main road. You have reached Grantchester. The Orchard Tea Garden, an excellent place to stop and have a cool drink, is a little way along the road to the left. To carry on with the main walk, turn right at the main road and continue until you reach the Green Man pub and a small village green. The Red Lion is a little further along the small road to the right, past the Green Man. At this point, the disabled will need to retrace their journey to return to Cambridge.

Carry on along the main road until you reach the Rupert Brooke pub on the right. Go to the extreme left-hand end of the pub's garden and car park and you will find a stile back into the meadows. Head straight ahead across the meadow until you reach the path once more. Turn left onto the path and retrace your steps as far as the city centre end of Granchester Street.

At this point, take the road to your right, at right-angles to Grantchester Street, with yellow lines along it. It is signposted 'The Granta Housing Trust'. Follow this road until you see an entrance to a car park on your right. Take the path in front of you through the barriers and over a black bridge. Carry on, veering slightly left along the path until you come to a junction of paths just before a boathouse. Take the left-hand path around the boathouse and continue alongside the river until you reach the main road.

Cross the road and turn right onto the pavement. Carry on along this road until you reach a set of roundabouts. Turn left at the first roundabout and the carry straight on along Trumpington Street. Follow Trumpington Street, passing the Fitzwilliam Museum, Peterhouse and Pembroke, until you reach the Pitt building once more. Retrace your steps along Trumpington Street and King's Parade to King's Porter's Lodge.

walk four: jesus, magdelene and open spaces

Facing King's Porter's Lodge, turn right along King's Parade. Soon you will notice Great St. Mary's Church, the University Church, on your right. Just after Great St. Mary's, go through the traffic barriers and turn left down Market Street. Carry on down Market Street, passing Cambridge's Market on your right.

Market Street veers sharply to the left, with a branch of Monsoon on its corner. Follow the road around. Its name will change to Sidney Street, but carry on straight ahead, past Sidney Sussex College on your right (p43) and the branch of Sainsbury's supermarket opposite. Soon after you have passed the entrance to Sidney Sussex, Sidney Street will come to the point at which a road comes in from the right and continues straight ahead.

Turn right down the road coming in from the right, Jesus Lane, crossing onto the left side of the road. Carry on along Jesus Lane until you reach some traffic lights. On your left is the ADC Theatre. The home of Cambridge's flourishing student drama scene, it shows two plays a week during term-time. Student actors and actresses at Cambridge are known as 'thesps' (from thespian), and are caricatured amongst

Jesus Green

undergraduates as insincere and exhibitionist. Nevertheless, Cambridge theatre is usually of a very high quality, and the ADC is definitely worth a visit.

Cross straight over the road and the traffic lights, and carry on along the left side of Jesus Lane for about 300 metres. Opposite the tall spire of the church on the right hand side of the road, you will notice a black wrought-iron gate to your left, and a long walled passage behind it. This is the entrance to Jesus College (p.30). The walkway is known as 'the chimney'.

If you are not visiting Jesus, carry on along Jesus lane another 200 metres until you reach a roundabout. Keeping to the left-hand side of the road, follow the pavement as it turns along Victoria Avenue, the first turning to the left out of the roundabout. Continue straight along this avenue of trees for about 300 metres, until you reach a pedestrian crossing where the road bends.

As you pass along Victoria Avenue, notice the green space to your right, on the other side of the road. This is Midsummer Common. The buildings on the far side of the common are college and university boathouses.

At the pedestrian crossing, turn left through some metal barriers onto a path across a park in front of you, Jesus Green. The path is another avenue of trees. Carry on straight ahead down the avenue, ignoring the path which crosses it half-way across Jesus Green, until you reach a bridge over the Cam and a lock. Turn left onto the path which follows the left bank of the Cam. After fifty or so metres, the path forks, with the tarmac veering off to the left and another path turning right, through some barriers, and keeping close to the Cam.

Take the right-hand path, moving onto a wooden walkway. Follow the walkway and the Cam until you reach Magdalene Bridge and Bridge Street.

If you wish to visit Magdalene College, or climb up Castle Mound, then turn right over Magdalene Bridge into Magdalene Street. About 30 metres along Magdalene Street, to the right as you go up it, is the entrance to Magdalene College (p.33). To get to Castle Mound, carry on up Magdalene Street. At the traffic lights, carry on straight up Castle Hill, on the right hand side of the road. After you pass the Castle Inn you will see a small path to the right. Take this path, which crosses the car park of Shire Hall, the large building to the left (the headquarters of Cambridgeshire County Council.) On the right, you will see Castle Mound and the path which leads up to it. Retrace your steps and carry on back over Magdalene Bridge onto Bridge Street. Ignore the next paragraph, and then follow the remainder of the walk back to King's.

If you wish to return to King's Parade, turn left at Magdalene Bridge, down Bridge Street.

Follow this road until you see St. John's Street off to the right, then turn into it. On your right, you will notice the immense edifice of St. John's College chapel, and further along, the entrance to the college (p41). Carry on along St. John's Street and you will come to Trinity College on your right (p44).

Continue along the same street, which has now become Trinity Street. You will pass Heffers, the city's most encyclopaedic bookshop, on your left, and some way further along, Gonville and Caius (pronounced "keys") College on your right (p.28). Carry on along Trinity Street until you see King's College Chapel over to the right as you reach the junction with St. Mary's Street. Cross over the road, through the barriers, and head up King's Parade, remaining on the left side of the road.

Carry on along King's Parade, and you will find yourself at King's College Porters' Lodge once more.

walk five: modern architecture

Famous for its old college buildings, Cambridge is also home to a host of modern architecture. The colleges' wealth, the continuing expansion of higher education, and Cambridge's burgeoning high-tech economy have brought many new buildings to the city. With space in the city centre at a premium, much of the University's growth has been in West Cambridge.

We begin outside the Mill public house. Just along Mill Lane is the imposing 'Grad Pad' or University Centre, housing bars and restaurants for graduate students and researchers. Across the river lies Darwin College Library (below), which makes the most of its riverbank location. Taking the alleyway past the Anchor and turning left onto Silver Street, we come to the main part of Darwin, including the small but impregnable porters' lodge and the long-legged octagonal Hall. Queens' Green, opposite, affords a view of Queens' new buildings, including the bar, gym, and multi-use Fitzpatrick Hall.

Sidgwick Avenue brings us to Newnham on the left, opposite the Sidgwick site, the closest the University currently comes to a central campus. Housing humanities departments, the core of the site was built in the early sixties and has been added to ever since. Nearer the road is the barn-like Classics Faculty, which houses the Museum of Classical Archaeology.

Sitting uneasily in the car park, slightly divorced from the other buildings, are two lecture theatres, Lady Mitchell Hall and the Little Hall. The latter looks every bit like a chapel, with a charming leaded spire. Up the wide steps, the central buildings of the site, stilted concrete blocks surrounding a grass square, are an unhappy marriage between an Oxbridge courtyard and a modern campus university.

Beyond this courtyard lies Norman Foster's gleaming new Law building. Sleek and sexy on the outside, the interior has been problematic in use, as has the neighbouring History Faculty. It's hard to believe History hasn't always looked dated, but it was acclaimed when new. A veritable ziggurat in red brick and glass, its rigid stepped form is quite a contrast with its younger neighbour. Overshadowed by History and Law, a surprisingly high-tech Divinity is just beginning to take shape at the time of writing.

The Music Faculty and West Road Concert Hall, which frequently holds public concerts, is nearly all roof. And a fine roof it is too; a striking geometric design in lead which sits well atop pale brick walls. It shares architects with nearby Caius' Harvey Court, which has a very similar feel.

Crossing West Road brings us to the University Library. Inspiring love, hate, fear, and loathing in those who use it, the enormous UL is certainly the city's most striking building. Having an undeniable grandeur and a certain ugly beauty, Sir George Gilbert Scott's creation has much in common with what is now the Tate Modern, which he also designed. Several extensions have been needed since its construction in the 1930s to accommodate an ever-growing number of books.

If you have tired of the modern already, now is an opportunity to turn right onto Burrell's Walk and head back into town. If not, turn left and proceed to the junction of Grange Road and Adams Road. To the left is Robinson, the youngest college. A fortress in red brick, Robinson's formidable exterior echoes medieval colleges' defensive aspect. The forbidding entrance even has a gatehouse tower, a drawbridge-like ramp, and the hint of a portcullis over the doorway.

On the right-hand side of Adams Road is Trinity Old Field, in the corner of which you can see the College's cricket pavillion (above) and squash courts. The large, but oddly quaint, Univerity Athletics club-house comes into view at the end of the road. The new Cavendish Laboratory, built in 1972 to house the Physics Department, is also just visible down the cyclepath. A new engineering department and Microsoft's computer laboratory are being built next door, part of the planned West Cambridge site.

The new maths department is on Wilberforce Road, past bauhaus-inspired houses and Emmanuel's charming cricket pavillion. A series of futuristic pagodas set around a central turf-roofed lecture theatre, the department has a very corporate feel. Next door, the Isaac Newton Institute for Mathematical Sciences was designed to increase interaction between researchers. There is even a blackboard in the lift.

Churchill College's Moller conference centre can be seen from the end of Wilberforce Road. A sight few undergraduates see (it's at least ten minutes' walk from the city centre) this ecclesiastically-inspired building (right) is truly remarkable, and from this distance appears alarmingly two-dimensional. The College's chapel is actually the rather drab little building to the left.

On the way down Clarkson Road, we pass Girton's Wolfson Court and, opposite, possibly the finest modern house in Cambridge, Number Three. Turning right down Grange Road returns us to Burrell's Walk, and hence the city centre. Here we come to Trinity Hall's riverside Wellcome Library (above), built in 1995 and a perfect example of how a well-planned modern building can complement its ancient surroundings. Finally, no tour of modern architecture in Cambridge would be complete without mention of the graceful Garret Hostel Bridge, on which you are now standing. Built in 1960, it was designed by a student of architecture at the University who died before its completion.

Other modern buildings worth seeing in Cambridge include St. John's Cripps Court, Wolfson's Lee Seng Tee Library on Barton Road, Kettles Yard Gallery, the Schlumberger building on Madingley Road, The Judge Institute of Management Studies on Trumpington Street, and the pedestrian railway bridge near the station.

Woolf

by the river

by the river

Walking is not the only way to see the beauty of Cambridge. In fact, on a hot summer's day there is no better way to view the colleges that line the Backs than drifting along in a punt.

Punting is the quintessence of the Cambridge myth – a handsome young man wearing boater and blazer guides his craft below the eight bridges, with a beautiful woman smiling up at him as he glides down the Cam. The picture almost holds true today, and although blazer and boater have given way to T-shirt and baseball cap, punting still remains one of the favourite ways for the Cambridge undergraduate to relax.

While most colleges don't hire their punts out to the public, it is possible for the visitor to hire a punt for the day or by the hour, with or without the services of an experienced punt-chauffeur, from one of the punt-hire companies operating along the river.

Punt-chauffeur services may offer anything from a full day's outing, complete with packed hamper and expert commentary on the sights, to little more than a competent hand on the pole. The more adventurous or athletic, however, may hire a punt by the hour from any of the jetties along the river, and do the driving for themselves.

lesson one: how to punt

Before you start, there are one or two preparations you can make. Don't wear clothing that could be stained by river water. Whilst punts are extremely difficult to capsize, it is very easy to fall out of one, especially if you are standing up. In addition, when handling the pole, water tends to run down your arm, so it is best to roll up your sleeves. Do wear shoes with good grips – if you have smooth soles, bare feet are probably a better bet.

Always stand squarely on the platform at the rear of the punt (the main difference between punting in Cambridge and Oxford: in the Other Place, the 'punter' stands at the front). If you feel insecure there, you can stand in the well behind the seats, thought this makes the punt harder to control. Try not to stand towards one side of the punt, as this will make it lean alarmingly.

The main problems that newcomers to punting face tend to centre on using the pole correctly. Hold the pole vertical directly at your side, with the end just above the water. Let it slip fast through your fingers, so that it hits the river bed. Holding with both hands, push downwards on the pole so that it tilts forwards. Make sure that the pole moves parallel to the punt – if it tilts at an angle, the punt will move to the side and swing round. If this happens, don't panic. Hold the pole so that it drags in the water behind the punt. Holding it at a shallow angle, half way out of the water, with your bottom hand quite low down the pole, use the pole as a rudder. If you point the pole to the left, the punt will move to the left, and vice versa. Once you're on course, pull the pole up and let it down as before, repeating the stroke to build up speed.

notorious pitfalls

• Don't attempt to get in a stroke before a bridge unless there are at least two full lengths of a punt in front of you. Poles are long things, and when they get jammed between the arch of a bridge and a river bed, you're in for trouble.

• Don't be tempted to hold onto the pole if it gets stuck in the river bed or against a bridge. Poles float, and can be retrieved by paddling back. If you hold on, the punt will drift onwards and you will slide off, clutching the pole. If you feel the pole sticking, twist it as you pull, but if it stays stuck, let it go!

• Beware of the deep areas under Magdalene Bridge (it's the big cast-iron road bridge next to Magdalene and St. John's Colleges). The river there is deeper than the length of some poles, so hang onto yours and just drift through.

where to go punting

There are two classic punting routes in Cambridge. The first is from Magdalene Bridge to Silver Street Bridge. This lasts about an hour, and takes you along the famous backs of the colleges, beneath all the bridges in the city centre. Especially beautiful is the stretch between St. John's Bridge of Sighs and Queens' Mathematical Bridge.

The other route is up-river from Silver Street to the delightful village of Grantchester. This lasts an afternoon and takes you through Grantchester Meadows, made famous by Rupert Brooke; you can moor at the bank there and picnic in pleasant surroundings, or buy a drink at one of the nearby pubs.

If you'd rather not punt, but would still like to catch some river action, you may be able to watch college boat crews training – or, at certain times of year, racing – on the river near Midsummer Common, where the college boathouses stand (see over page).

A Newnham Ladies' Crew in action

punt companies

All punt companies require a deposit on hire punts. Chauffeur punt trips vary in length, between 40 minutes and an hour for going along the backs, and are longer (and dearer) for going up river towards Grantchester.

Scudamore's Punting Company
Quayside (Magdalene Bridge)
and Mill Lane (by the Mill Pub).
Tel: 01223 359750
www.scudamores.co.uk

Granta Punt Hire
The Granta Inn, Newnham Mill Pond
Tel: 01223 301845

Trinity College Punt Hire
Garret Hostel Lane
Tel: 01223 338483

Cambridge Chauffeur Punts
Silver Street Bridge
Tel: 01223 354164/359299

where to go

where to go

Cambridge has a lot to offer beyond the confines of the college courts. The city has a long and complex history of its own, and this is reflected in the enormous variety of buildings and its twisting medieval passageways and lanes. There is much to do and see around Cambridge. Here is a selection of the essentials.

Guided Tours
The best way for big groups to see the major sights is by taking a guided tour with one of the registered blue-badged guides, as many of the big colleges require large groups to be accompanied. Go to the Tourist Information Centre to sign up.

Bus Tours
Tickets and information from Guide Friday at Cambridge Railway Station. Tel: 01223 362444
Tours of the city, taking in the American Cemetery at Madingley, run regularly. Bus tours, which include a commentary on the sights, are a good way for a visitor in a hurry to see the city.

Walking Tours
Tickets and information from the Tourist Information Centre, Wheeler Street. Tel: 01223 322640
Tours go very regularly in the summer, and twice daily in the winter months, departing from the Information Centre. They include visits to college grounds, with an informed commentary from a trained guide.

where to go: theatre in cambridge

the importance of being earnest at the adc theatre

theatre in cambridge

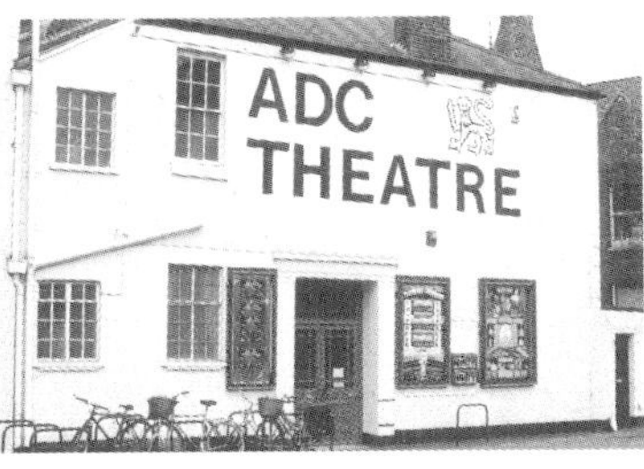

Most well-known, in student terms, is the ADC Theatre (bookings via the Arts' box office on 01223 503333) on Park Street. The Footlights perform their annual pantomime and Spring and Summer Revues here, as well as regular 'Smokers' throughout term, where new material is tried out. Aside from comedy, the ADC is the venue for two shows weekly, running Mon-Sat at 8pm (the main-show, usually the work of an established playwright) and 11pm (the lateshow, often more light-hearted and experimental).

For those with more limited funds, working as an usher allows you to see a performance for free, but places for each show are

a streetcar named desire at the adc theatre

limited, so you need to be quick signing up. The theatre bar is a renowned meeting-place for University thesps, and the student bar staff will be able to let you know who's tipped for the top in Cambridge drama.

The recently renovated Arts Theatre (01223 503333) on Peas Hill (just off Market Square) is the main professional venue, and hosts a wide variety of touring drama, dance, and opera productions, with one-off comedy and music nights during each season.

Stephen Fry is rumoured to have been instrumental in setting up the Playroom, on St. Edward's Passage (off King's Parade), a small venue with an experimental L-shaped auditorium. Run by Corpus Christi's Fletcher Players, the Playroom is particularly good for plays that require an immediacy with the audience.

The Cambridge Drama Centre (01223 322748), in Covent Garden (off Mill Road), is a small professional theatre, hosting mainly new work from up-and-coming touring companies, whilst the Junction, further out of town off Clifton Road, also stages dance and theatre alongside its more usual repertoire of club nights and concerts.

The Corn Exchange (01223 357851) lies on Wheeler Street and attracts professional and semi-professional shows from around the country. One of the few really big venues in Cambridge, major shows and comedians regularly make the trek up from London or stop here on tour. Since the Corn Exchange also doubles as a straightforward musical venue, it is not uncommon to find theatre with a strongly tuneful element on the bill.

A number of individual colleges have their own purpose-built theatres or auditorium space that doubles as a theatre venue. Homerton, the only college where drama can be found on the curriculum, has a great studio, and student shows can often reward those who venture outside the centre of town. Likewise, Robinson's modern theatre is worth leaving the beaten track for. CADS, the Christ's dramatic society, have their own theatre within college grounds, as do Queens' with their luxurious Fitzpatrick Hall (complete with motorised stage). The Emmanuel College Queen's Building has a open, balconied, semi-circular stage area that provides an alternative to the proscenium arches found elsewhere in town.

Of course, in May Week anything goes as far as theatre venues are concerned, and plays pop up in college gardens all over Cambridge. Many of the commonly used locations (such as Queens' Cloister Court, Sidney Sussex and Clare Gardens and the gorgeous grounds of Newnham) offer beautiful settings for fun-filled afternoon and early evening performances, with Shakespearean comedies at the heart of the repertoire.

The Queens' College Fitzpatrick Hall, a popular venue for student theatre

cambridge cinema

A Cambridge student has three sorts of cinema experience to choose from. Firstly, the multiplex experience provided by the Warner Village at the Grafton Centre. With eight screens, digital sound and online ticket sales (www.warnervillage.co.uk), it is of the high quality you'd expect, but is really no different from any other Warner Village Cinema across the UK. For the more discerning viewer with an interest in art-house films, the brand-new Arts Picturehouse (www.picturehouse-cinemas.co.uk/cb/) offers an excellent alternative. Comprising three screens and a stylish bar for customers' use, it is (in)conveniently located above the largest pub in the UK.

However, from a student perspective, the most enjoyable (and wallet-friendly) cinema experience is provided by college film societies. About half a dozen colleges boast a student-run cinema, ranging from a cosy room showing classics and old favourites to a 250-seater auditorium, with 35mm projector and Dolby Digital Surround Sound, showing many of the latest blockbusters. Student film societies also have showings of the latest films from the University's film societies, where you can see up-and-coming student talent in action. Details of films and venues can be found in the weekly Varsity listings pages (in the paper or online at www.varsity.cam.ac.uk), or on the college film society websites, linked from their host college sites.

museums and galleries

Sadly overlooked by many visitors to the city, Cambridge boasts a remarkable number and variety of museums and galleries. Many are run by the University for the benefit of students, and most are open to the public free of charge.

The imposing classical bulk of the Fitzwilliam Museum (below) on Trumpington Street houses the University's extensive collection of art and antiquities. One of the finest art museums in the country outside London, the Fitz has a large collection of paintings on display in the upper galleries including old masters, French impressionists, and a number of fine 20th century works. The lower galleries house antiquities from ancient Greece, Rome, and Egypt in addition to applied arts from around the world and a fearful display of medieval arms and armour.

In addition to the permanent collections, there are usually three temporary exhibitions on view at any one time. The museum runs many activities around the exhibitions including guided tours, children's workshops, talks and lectures, as well as a series of afternoon and evening concerts. There is a well-stocked shop and a cafe.

Open: Tues-Sat 10am-5pm Sun 2.15-5pm. Free.

The truly incomparable Kettle's Yard (below; Castle Street) is neither a museum nor an art gallery; it's a way of life. Originally the home of Jim Ede, former Tate curator, the house displays the fine collection of modern art he gave to the University in a unique domestic setting. Sculpture by Henry Moore and Henri Gaudier-Brzeska and paintings by Ben Nicholson, Alfred Wallis, and William Congdon among others fill this remarkable building alongside more everyday objects. The result is a gallery like no other, intended as a "refuge of peace and order, of visual arts and of music."

Adjoining the house is the more recently added gallery, a wonderful naturally-lit space which is at once intimate and spacious. The gallery shows a wide range of exhibitions of contemporary art, which are accompanied by talks and educational activities for all age groups. If you go nowhere else in Cambridge, go to Kettle's Yard. In the words of its founder Jim Ede, "there should be a Kettle's Yard in every university."

Open: house – Tues-Sun 2-4pm; gallery – Tues-Sat 12.30-5.30pm; Sun 2-5.30pm. Free.

The University Museum of Zoology (Downing St.) is hard to miss thanks to the 70-foot Finback Whale skeleton above the door. Inside, smaller cetaceans hang above a bewildering array of all things that walk, fly, crawl or swim. Prehistoric fish, giant spider crabs, pickled squid, an extinct aurochs dug up from the fens, the largest living salamander, and the skeleton of Polymelus, one of the greatest progenitors of the modern thoroughbred horse, are just a few of the attractions in this fascinating, well laid-out museum.

Open: Mon-Fri 10am-1pm & 2-4.45pm (afternoons only during term). Free.

The Museum of Archaeology and Anthropology (Downing Street) is home to a wealth of material from around the globe, covering Africa, Asia, the Pacific and pre-Columbian America as well as ancient Britain.

Open: Tues-Sat 2-4.30pm. Free.

The University's oldest museum in more ways than one, the Sedgwick Museum of Earth Sciences (background picture; Downing Street) was founded in 1728 and houses an incredible one million fossils, some up to three billion years old, including an iguanadon, an ancient hippopotamus excavated just a few miles away at Barrington, and the largest ever spider.

Open: Mon-Fri 9am-1pm & 2-5pm; Sat 10am-1pm. Free.

A fascinating collection of scientific instruments and apparatus, the Whipple Museum of the History of Science (Free School Lane) houses everything from sundials to pocket calculators under an Elizabethan hammer-beam roof which dates back to 1618.

Open: Mon-Fri 1.30-4.30pm. Free.

The Museum of Classical Archaeology (Sidgwick Avenue) is part of the Classics Faculty, boasting one of the world's largest collections of plaster casts of Greek and Roman statues.

Open: Mon-Fri 9am-5pm. Fre.

The Scott Polar Research Institute (Lensfield Road), a memorial to Captain R. F. Scott and his ill-fated expedition, is one of the world's leading centres for polar research. Its museum documents both the history of polar exploration and current research.

Open: Mon-Sat 2.30-4pm. Free.

The vast University Library (West Road) is one of the largest working libraries in the world. A recently-opened exhibition centre allows the public to see a small fraction of its treasures in a series of exhibitions which run for six months at a time.

Open: Mon-Fri 9am-6pm; Sat 9am-12.30pm. Free.

The Cambridge Darkroom (Gwydir Street) is dedicated to photography, especially encouraging new talent. In addition to exhibitions, the Darkroom runs talks and courses on all aspects of the art and provides darkroom space (what else?) for developing amateur photographers.

Open: Tues-Sun 12-5pm. Free.

Next to Kettle's Yard, the Cambridge and County Folk Museum (Catsle Street) is full of artefacts from the past few hundred years of Cambridge's history, including an entire 18th century shop front.

Open: Mon-Sat 10.30am-5pm; Sun 2-5pm. £2 (children 50p, concs £1)

Formerly a Victorian pumping station on the banks of the Cam, the Cambridge Museum of Technology (Cheddars Lane) shows exhibits from the city's industrial past, including a steam engine which can occasionally be seen working.

Open: Sun 2-5pm. £2 (£4 if in steam)

churches

Cambridge has many picturesque and ancient churches which are well worth visiting. A few are as old as the city itself, and many are remarkably beautiful.

St. Bene't's Church (St Benedict's), Bene't Street
St Bene't's Saxon tower is the oldest building in Cambridge. It was probably built around 1025, while the nave was rebuilt in the 13th century. Other parts were added in the 14th and 15th centuries, including the gallery connecting the church with neighbouring Corpus Christi College. St. Bene't's served as Corpus' Chapel for over 300 years.

St. Edward, King and Martyr, St. Edward's Passage
This church, tucked away behind King's Parade, is dedicated to the Saxon king Edward the Confessor. Most of the building dates from the 15th century, although the tower is probably 12th century. The aisles were built around 1450 by Trinity Hall and Clare Hall, to serve as college chapels after their local church was pulled down to make way for King's College.

Little St. Mary's Church, Trumpington Street
The church was originally dedicated to St. Peter, and acted as chapel for Peterhouse until 1632. It was rebuilt and re-dedicated to the Virgin Mary in 1350. Near the entrance is a memorial to Godfrey Washington, who died in 1729, a fellow of Peterhouse and relative of George Washington. The memorial

includes the Washington crest of three stars and stripes surmounted by an eagle, which was the basis for the flag of the United States of America.

Great St. Mary's, the University Church,
King's Parade

The present church was built in 1478 to replace an earlier 14th century one. Formerly known as 'St. Mary's by the Market', it is still used for some University ceremonies, and the University sermon is preached there every Sunday evening during term. The church is also the starting-point from which the first milestones in Britain were measured: undergraduates are still required to live within three miles of it in order to count 'in residence'. If nine terms are not spent within these boundaries, then the student cannot graduate. The tower of the church, which was built in 1608, is usually open to the public, and provides panoramic views over the city.

The Round Church (Holy Sepulchre Church),
Round Church Street

One of Cambridge's most popular tourist sites, this is one of the very few churches in Britain to be built with a circular nave (background picture), in commemoration of the Holy Sepulchre in Jerusalem. It was erected in 1130, and the chancel and north aisle were rebuilt in the 15th century. The present roof is a 19th century replacement for the original 15th century polygonal bell-tower, which was removed during the course of restoration work carried out by Anthony Salvin in 1841.

parks and gardens

Milton Country Park

Where to find it: Cambridge Road, Milton – take Cambus service 109 or 124 from Drummer Street Bus Station.

A little-known getaway from Cambridge city centre, Milton Country Park has plenty to offer. Just a short bus ride from Cambridge, and with free entrance every day of the year, it's a wonder that more people haven't discovered the beauty of the Park's lakes, woods and wildlife. Upon entrance, the Visitor Centre contains a wealth of leaflets, information and displays about interesting sights to look out for, ranging from migrating birds and Muntjac deer to the resident swans and geese. Spanning some 85 acres of extensively landscaped former quarry, the Park makes considerable contributions to conservation efforts. Its main attractions are its two large lakes, with two miles of footpaths surrounding them (also accessible by wheelchair and bicycle). Bird lovers will be especially rewarded, with dozens of species choosing the Park as their habitat. The friendly Park Rangers are always willing to answer any questions and can organise activities for groups and schools. All in all, Milton Country Park makes for a perfect Easter term outing.

More details can be found at:
http://www.scambs.gov.uk/Scambs/tourism.nsf/pages/miltonpark.html

Cambridge University Botanic Gardens

Where to find it: Cory Lodge, Bateman Street (off Hills Road)

The only sizeable park actually in Cambridge, the Botanic Gardens were originally created for the purpose of research. Although still a place of research, they appeals strongly to visitors, due to their sheer scale and variety of plant life as well as the close proximity to the centre of Cambridge. It is surprising how peaceful the Gardens appear from within, compared with the bustle of traffic a mere five minutes' walk away. The Gardens' park-like nature and diversity, including the winter and rock gardens, make a visit worthwhile at any time of year. There are also many species of birds nesting in the gardens and lake, which are detailed on the Gardens' notice board, along with other current sights of interest. Don't miss the sensory explosion of the scented garden, as well as the glass houses, full of alpine, tropical and even flesh-eating plants. On a typical summer's day you could find families wandering with their children, students relaxing and revising, and tourists sampling the most natural attraction Cambridge has to offer.

More details can be found at:
http://www.plantsci.cam.ac.uk/Botgdn
Email: gardens@hermes.cam.ac.uk

There are also many lovely open spaces around the city centre. Jesus Green, between Jesus College and the Cam (accessed from Bridge Street, Chesterton and Victoria) is the largest, offers a delightful riverside walk and is an ideal spot for picnics. Just across Victoria Avenue is Midsummer Common, where the city's spectacular Guy Fawkes Night fireworks display is held every November. The Midsummer Fair, held annually on the common, has roots in medieval times. This is also where farmers graze their cattle, and cows have been known to tumble into the waters of the Cam, sparking off extensive rescue operations to return them to dry land. Parker's Piece, located between Regent Street and Parkside, is cynically known as 'reality checkpoint' as it is felt that this marks the south-eastern boundary between Town and Gown.

Sheep's Green (accessed by the bridge at the end of Mill Lane) is a favourite place to stop and picnic, as it is right next to the Mill Pub, and close to the river. Lammas Land is a little further along the towpath and can be somewhat quieter during the summer. A little further afield are the wide expanses of Grantchester Meadows (see the Walks section).

It should be noted that colleges discourage picknickers in their grounds. However, there are grassy areas along the Backs that lend themselves to a pleasant break from the bustle of the centre of town. At the end of the summer term, some colleges' Fellows' Gardens are open to the public under the National Gardens Scheme.

music

The musical repertoire of Cambridge is wide and varied. Student jazz and swing bands perform regularly in college bars, while the Boat Race Pub (background picture), on Burleigh Street near the Grafton Centre, has a varied selection of bands seven nights a week (01223 360873). For the classically inclined, the University Music Society performs orchestral and choral works regularly at the University's West Road Concert Hall (below). To find out what is being performed by college-based orchestral groups, ask at Porters' Lodges, or check the weekly listings in Varsity, the student newspaper. Perhaps the most well-known is King's College Chapel Choir, who can be heard during services in the College Chapel. Contact the Porters' Lodge at King's for details on 331100. The most versatile, all-round venue for music in Cambridge is the Corn Exchange in Wheeler Street, (01223 337851), behind the Market Square, which has in the past attracted artists from the Bolshoi Ballet to the Manic Street Preachers. Tickets are best booked in advance from the box office.

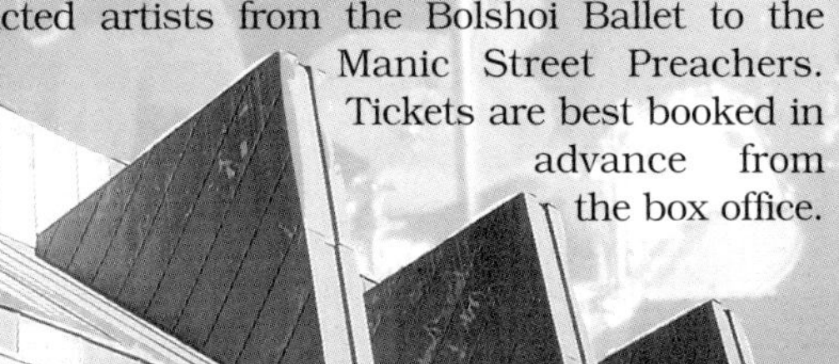

nightlife

Although incomparable to larger cities such as London or Sheffield, Cambridge's 'Club Scene' is certainly buzzing, with a number of popular venues around the city. Fifth Avenue Nightclub (01223 364222) in Lion Yard is the centre of student nightlife, still known to most by its former name 'Cindy's' and renowned for its 'cheesy' music. Just outside of town, the Junction (01223 511511) on Clifton Road caters for music of many different styles, as do Kambar on Wheeler Street

(01223 842725) and the Q Club on Station Road (01223 315466).

The Corn Exchange (01223 337851) also holds all-night dance events, most recently featuring top DJs from Miss Moneypenny's and Radio One. On a smaller scale, the Chicago Rock Café (01223 324600), situated just off Sidney Street, and Bar Coast on the Quayside near Magdalene Bridge are also popular. Both boast large bars and big sound-systems, although the dance floors are much smaller.

shopping

If you're after a quick spot of retail therapy, Cambridge is small, but perfectly formed. There is something in this city to suit every taste and purse. For people dressing to impress, must-see shops include Jigsaw, Morgan, Karen Millen and Phase Eight. For those with an allowance, the city is crammed with tiny, exclusive designer shops, notably Troon (King's Parade), Jane (Sussex Street), Hero (Green Street), Giulio and BlueMax (both King Street) – and, to top off that perfect outfit, the not-to-be-missed Baska Design hat and accessories shop on Magdalene Street.

For the guys there are great places to get suited and booted: if you're looking for that must-have tux and can stretch to a new one, the Savoy Taylors' Guild on St. John's Street is a blast from the past. These tailors will work with you to find something that 'really, ooh, suits you.' Similarly, Austin Reed, found on Sidney Street, offers suits for all occasions. Slightly more grant-friendly are Next, Top Man and French Connection, variously dotted about the pedestrianised city centre.

For the girls, high-street smart is represented by all the major names: Next, Top Shop, Miss Selfridge, Oasis, Kookai, Warehouse, French Connection and Monsoon. For underwear there's an M&S or, if you can stretch to it, La Senza has exciting undies secreted in the Grafton Centre. Even more luxurious is Le Reve on Bene't Street – only for the extremely hedonistic. Many of the chain-names are to be found nestling in the city centre, with more of the same and a few storming shoeshops out at the Grafton Centre.

For the hippys, freaks and weirdos out there, heartily recommended are Mayhem (Sidney Street), Cult Clothing (Sidney Street) and Sunrise (Burleigh Street). Burleigh Street, a whole eight minutes walk from the town centre, is located next to the Grafton Centre and Sunrise is the place in Cambridge for PVC, leather, and hippy kit. It also does a nice sideline in funky jewellery and a cabinet full of cigarette papers and smoking paraphanalia.

Strawberry Fayre, which usually hits town in Mayweek, is Cambridge's answer to Glastonbury and a one-day wonder. Stalls selling everything and anything will pop up on Midsummer Common and it's a great chance to get cut-price combats, clubbing gear and more way-out stuff.

If you're a fan of all things phat, try Dogfish on Green Street and Cult Clothing (Sidney Street). A word of warning, however: don't bother going into Cult Clothing with that old Aran 'V'-neck jumper and the comfy cords that you slouch around in – you're way uncool and probably don't deserve to be told where the shop is. Seriously, this place has pretensions of cool that are generally met by the clothes, clientele, staff and a soundtrack that booms out into the Cambridge air like a beacon of cool.

Cambridge's greatest shopping claim to fame must lie with thrift-shop chic. We're bubbling over with charity shops offering great second hand stuff that the groovy cats of the 60s, 70s and 80s have finally thrown away. Burleigh Street up by the Grafton Centre is the Mecca for bargain hunters with an eye for style. Scope, Cancer Research, the Heart Foundation and Mind offer the best bargains while Oxfam offers a range of second hand and new goods for sale. Hills Road also has much to offer in this line, while Mill Road boasts a few great charity shops, the largest of which is the Salvation Army shop. A tip from an old hand – Scope is the place to seek out the most sumptuous second hand deals.

presents and decor

For anything from the sublime to the ridiculous, head for Green Street and Rose Crescent: Chaps (Green Street) offers perfect bizarro pressies ranging from the rude or silly to just damn stylish gifts such as chocolate nipples, novelty toilet seats or lava lamps. Also on Green Street lie a tiny shop specialising in filofax equipment and Past Times, specialising in, well, past times! Wow (Rose Crescent) offers funky knick-knacks, cooking and cocktail items. Evolution (Fitzroy Street) offers lovely room-decorating kit from throws and cushions to oil burners, lamps and Fengshui bits and bobs and objet d'arts that all aesthetes will love and most will be able to afford. Spoils, the Kitchen Reject Shop on Sussex Street (and also in the Grafton Centre) is another great place to go for presents and for setting your room up. As its name suggests, they do cutlery, crockery and glasses in addition to bead curtains, throws, beanbags and cushions, which are all cheap and cheerful.

music

HMV (Lion Yard), Virgin (Grafton Centre) and Andy's Records (Fitzroy Street) provide the soundtracks to life. In addition, a pretty good selection of specialist shops is to be found on King Street. All tiny, their characters are to be identified by the noises spilling out into the street: gut-churningly dark drum'n'bass, choice tunes of present and past at a cut price rate (Parrot Records), and jazz and classical tunes with mind-blowing cadenzas. For classical there are also specialist shops on Green Street and Trinity Street.

food

If you eat to live, Sainsbury's on Sidney Street is a must. Aside from the good but pricey M&S foodhall on Market Square, Sainsbury's is the only regular supermarket in the centre. Shoppers are guaranteed to bump into every student in town on each visit, so it's known amongst students as a great place to meet your mates. If you're more of the 'live to eat' nature, the Cambridge Cheese Company on All Saints' Passage and the Eaden Lilley Food Hall on Sussex Street are places to frequent. The CCC (above) sells cheeses to die for in addition to amazing olives, meats and sundries that have to be tasted to be believed!

For drink, most students will pay frequent visits to well-endowed college wine cellars, where wine is often top-quality and better value than from the city's off-licences. Those who don't have access to such luxuries – or who prefer beer and spirits – Oddbins, Bottoms Up or Threshers are only ever a short walk away.

bookshops

Students = books, and Cambridge is no exception. 15,000 students at two universities, and a day trip's worth of bookshops. The University Press has its own, at the end of King's Parade, which, like Marks and Spencer, only stocks own-brand items. If you're after something that boasts the University logo but is more interesting than a sweatshirt, that's the place to go. A wider selection can be found at the legendary Heffers, just down the road on Trinity Street. Although it's now run by Blackwell's, the main shop still overflows with books on every subject, from fly-fishing to film-making, with a healthy fiction section in between.

Back in the centre of town, Sidney Street boasts four bookshops, with two branches of Waterstones, and Galloway and Porter's – the best place to go for those on a budget. As well as remaindered books, they have an extensive second-hand section, and an Everything-for-£1 section outside. Quality and quantity. If you want to feel good while you read, there's the Oxfam bookshop two doors away, with cheap books and their own range of chocolate – a perfect combination. For that fuzzy feeling, you could also try the Amnesty International book shop on Mill Road. As you're walking back towards town, you'll come across CB1, a secondhand bookstore and internet café, where you can browse over a cappuccino. Its sister shop CB2, near the Warner Village cinema, keeps serving – and selling books –

until late.

Market Square, though, is the book lover's Mecca. There's always a book stall in the market – look out for Alister & Garon, among whose tables there are guaranteed to be some bizarre buys that make perfect gifts. They also have a shop on King Street which sells second-hand vinyl and CDs as well. If you're after old books, G. David is the place to go. Hidden in St. Edward's Passage (along the side of the Arts Theatre), this is one for the cognoscenti. Outside, there are racks of books for 50p – but check out the window. I'm reliably informed that at one point this summer, it held a first edition of Paradise Lost (for a cool £14,000) It's Cambridge's friendliest book store, so worth the visit even if you only leave with a 50p paperback.

And opposite G. David (pictured left), there is a bookshop for those, like Alice, who like their books with pictures. The Haunted Bookshop specialises in children's books that are adults' pleasures – lavishly-illustrated first editions of your childhood favourites. Prices aren't for the squeamish. If you're really on a quest to spend, head for Granta Books on Castle Hill, and thrill to the smell of old leather and parchment. American giants Borders are threatening to open in Market Square. Ignore them, and discover that Cambridge bookshops have a charm all of their own.

out of town

There is more to Cambridgeshire than just the city of Cambridge. The area round about has a rich cultural heritage, and if you have a few days to spend, you could do worse than escape the bustle of the town centre and range further afield. There follow just a few of the best sights and sites.

near cambridge

Closest of all the delightful villages clustered around Cambridge is Grantchester (see walk three, p.73, for more details). Between Grantchester and the neighbouring village of Trumpington lies Byron's Pool, a pond where the poet often bathed whilst an undergraduate at Trinity College.

Three miles west of Cambridge along the A1303 lies the quiet village of Madingley. Near the village is the 16th-century Madingley Hall where the fleeing Charles I stayed, now the base of the University's Board of Continuing Education (01954 280280): you too can spend time here whilst participating in one of their many and varied summer courses. England's only American Military Cemetery (01954 210350) is also located nearby: open daily, the cemetery's hauntingly landscaped grounds provide the resting place for 3,811 American servicemen, who died while operating from British bases during World War II. Its Memorial Wall carries the names of 5,215 servicemen whose graves are unknown.

Ancient earthworks can be found on Cambridge's Gog Magog Hills (two miles south of the city along the A1307). Wandlebury Ring is the remains of a 1st century Iron-Age hill fort. The building in its centre is the stable block of a 18th-century mansion; it covers the grave of the horse Godolphin Arab, forebear of many English racehorses, who was buried there in 1753.

Just on the edge of the tiny village of Lode, five miles north-east of Cambridge along the B1102, stands Anglesey Abbey (01223 811200), a beautiful mansion built in the 1590s on the site of a 12th century Augustinian priory. Owners have included Sir George Downing, founder of Downing College in Cambridge, and Lord Fairhaven, whose art collections are displayed throughout the house, and who created the spectacular 100-acre Georgian-style grounds.

further afield

Jungle Book fans should be prepared for the 25-minute drive to the former home of Kipling's daughter, Wimpole Hall (01223 207257; nine miles to the south-west along the A603). Started in 1640, the house was completed in the 18th century, and the grounds were landscaped by Capability Brown in 1770. The landscaping involved the complete demolition of the original village of Wimpole, rehoused at New Wimpole, along the main road.

Nearer Cambridge at Duxford Airfield (8 miles south of Cambridge, off Junction 10 on the M11; there are also regular free buses from the railway station in

See planes at Duxford Airfield

Cambridge) is the Imperial War Museum (01223 834973). Lurking in the hangars are more than 100 aircraft, ranging from crude bi-planes to the prototype Concorde. For the intrepid, flights around the airfield are sometimes on offer, and there's always the consolation of the flight simulator for those who want to do the driving. The museum also has exhibitions featuring midget submarines and other fascinating details of military developments over the last hundred years.

For those who prefer leopards to weaponry, a visit to Linton Zoo (01223 891308) is a must. Ten miles south-east of Cambridge along the A1307, the ten-acre family-run zoo houses bears, owls, lynxes, the rare Indian eagle owl and the binturong (a long-haired Asian mammal), all in well-maintained grounds.

A little further afield (fifteen miles south along the A130) is the beautiful medieval town of Saffron Walden. Its name is taken from the Saffron crocus, grown here for its orange dye until late last century, which appears on the town's coat of arms. The town also benefited greatly from the wool trade, and its imposing church bears witness to its wealth and prosperity during medieval times. The town's many surviving 16th century houses boast striking displays of 'pargetting' (ornamental plasterwork), especially in Church Street. One mile west of Saffron Walden stands the magnificent 17th century Jacobean Audley End House (01799 522842). Originally three times its present size, it was dubbed by James I as "too large for a king". The interiors have benefited from the talents of Sir John Vanbrugh and Robert Adam, while the gardens were landscaped by Capability Brown. Rides are often available on a miniature railway which runs round the grounds.

Fifteen miles east of Cambridge along the A45 and

A11 lies the county's horseracing Mecca, Newmarket. Races have been held at the town since the first gold cup race in 1635, and the full story can be had at the National Horse-Racing Museum on the High Street (01638 667333). For the less horsey, there is the seven-mile Devil's Dyke, a 6th century earthwork built to defend the Saxon inhabitants from hostile tribes to the south.

Ely (sixteen miles north-east along the A10) is best known for its spectacular 12th and 14th century Cathedral. Its remarkable octagonal tower can be seen for miles across the Fens, and seeing it gives sense to the old name 'the Isle of Ely', which dates from when the Fens where covered by sea and the town was an island. Also in Ely Cathedral is the Stained Glass Museum (01353 660347). The town was once home to Oliver Cromwell, and more can be discovered at the Ely Museum (01353 666655), just north of the Cathedral.

Huntingdon (16 miles north-west along the A604) was once the county town of the now abolished Huntingdonshire. It was also the birthplace of Oliver Cromwell, and the Cromwell Museum provides a record of his life. It is housed in a former grammar school, at which both Cromwell and the diarist Samuel Pepys were pupils. Not far to the west of Huntingdon stands Hinchingbrooke House, a 16th century mansion which was once home to a branch of the Cromwell family. Built on the site of a defunct Augustinian nunnery, it is now a school, but is often open to visitors, with senior pupils acting as guides.

eating out

restaurant guide
:posh nosh

Cambridge bursts at the seams with great places to eat. It has the generic chain restaurants in abundence. From Café Uno and Café Rouge to the burger bars and pizza restaurants, all major brand names are well represented. We focus below on some restaurants unique to Cambridge.

Bangkok City
24 Green Street,
01223 354382

For Thai food in Cambridge, it doesn't get any better than the centrally located Bangkok City. Delicious dishes come piled high: these are ample servings for the hungry. A request ensures your dishes are as spicy as required and the flavours and textures of Thailand are echoed in the decor. Elegant and wonderfully East Asian. A place usually brimming with academics and the more affluent (or debt-ridden) students.

Bar Ha! Ha!
Trinity Street

A new clientele have regained this part of Trinity Street. Gone is the Blue Boar, home of Americana and gas station trinkets: here is a thoroughly modern bar-restaurant. The food, however, is what sets Bar Ha! Ha! apart, and tantalisingly-described dishes such as Plump Pumpkin Tortellini and Bangers with Mustard Mash are very good value for money.

Browns
23 Trumpington Street, 01223 461655

Browns (below) offers excellent quality food, smart service and elegant surroundings. At the beginning of any term and in late June when Graduation ceremonies take place, students and proud parents flock here in large numbers. While the meat eater is more than adequately catered for, this restaurant seems reluctant to expand its vegetarian menu; the few vegetarian dishes they do offer are perfectly pleasant. This restaurant remains a favourite for those seeking something a bit special, particularly when the parents are paying!

Cambridge Lodge Hotel and Restaurant
Huntingdon Road, 01223 352833

An excellent, relaxed country-house style restaurant with a wide-ranging and individual menu. Situated close to Fitz and New Hall, and hence a bit of a trek, relatively speaking, from town, there is ample car parking available. For those lucky students with generous parents, this is high on the wish-list when the topic of lunch on graduation day comes around.

Chato Singapore Restaurant
2-4 Lensfield Road, 01223 364115

Often surprisingly quiet, particularly at lunchtime, this Singaporian restaurant offers large portions for relatively large prices. The quality is usually pretty high and the set menu dishes offer the best deal. If you enjoy the flavours of Asia you won't go far wrong here.

Hobbs Pavilion
Parker's Piece, 01223 367480
Closed Sunday and Monday

At Easter time, this place really comes into its own. The Cadbury's Cream Egg pancake is divine – and more chocolately than anyone can handle alone! This pavilion-style restaurant, overlooking Parker's Piece, specialises in crepes, both savoury and wickedly sweet. Truly unique to Cambridge, and named after the legendary cricketer, Hobbs will hit you for six. The food makes for an unusual alternative, especially for vegetarians bored with pasta. A particular must for anyone with a sweet tooth.

marketplace shopping

Not all Cambridge waiters look like this: ballgoers at Robinson's 'Ritmo Latino' Ball 2000 enjoy being served food by spectacularly-costumed garçons

Le Jardin
The Garden House Hotel, Granta Place, Mill Lane, 01223 259988

Le Jardin is an elegant restaurant boasting an extensive range of high-quality cuisine including imaginative vegetarian options. The food is beautifully presented, and the staff wonderfully attentive. The atmosphere is formal; this is the perfect place to come, eat and feel part of the Cambridge elite! The chances are that if you can afford it you'll love it.

Loch Fyne Restaurant
Trumpington Street, 01223 362433

The Loch Fyne experience is a refreshing one; the fresh idea of situating a fish restaurant in Cambridge, the fresh, airy pinewood interior and fresh, fresh oysters. This is a foodie's paradise, offering an extensive menu with a well chosen wine list, and (as is necessary with the fluctuating seasonal quality of some shellfish) extremely knowledgeable and courteous staff. Many items on the menu are not cheap (you would not get much change out of £20 a head), but this is rare quality well worth paying for.

Michel's Brasserie and Wine Bar
22-24 Northampton Street, 01223 353110

A French restaurant with elegance and flair, Michel's is a great alternative to the pseudo-Gallic offerings of the various chain brasseries.

Midsummer House
Midsummer Common, 01223 368299

Midsummer House is a gastranomic experience to savour, and unless you are blessed with a very understanding bank manager, one you will not be enjoying very often. This is haute cuisine, par exellence. With tables situated in the individual rooms of this Victorian house, there are minimal distractions from the food, just a reverent silence accompanying every beautifully crafted course. The wine list runs to twenty-seven pages and caters for every nuance of this culinary symphony. Under the management of Tony Rios it can only be a matter of time before they receive their well-deserved Michelin star.

Panos Hotel and Restaurant
Hills Road, 01223 212958

The Panos Hotel is an interesting fusion of French and Greek style, and for the most part they manage to maintain the delicate flavours, without transgressing into over-richness. The emphasis here is on hospitality, and Geneiveve, the proprietress, makes her genial presence felt throughout the evening, and over a course of anything from escargot to swordfish kebab, one feels, for a brief moment, part of the family. For the quality of the cuisine (if not the interior) this is well worth a trip to the outer reaches of Cambridge city centre.

The Peking
21 Burleigh Street, 01223 354755

The Peking is a small family-owned Chinese restaurant with astonishingly good food. If your idea of a chinese restaurant is the take-away, think again. This is high-quality cuisine bursting with exquisite and delicate flavours. The quality comes at a price, but the portions are very generous. Service is exceptionally friendly, though not intrusive for those wanting a quiet meal. The surroundings are basic compared with the sumptuous and ostentatious splendour of some of the other eateries of Cambridge, but, nestling between shops on Burleigh Street, this little restaurant is a gem.

Restaurant 22
22 Chesterton Road, 01223 351880
Closed Sunday and Monday

Reputedly one of the best restaurants in Cambridge, 22 doesn't disappoint! Serving first-class and imaginative English food (no, not, as many would fear, a contradiction in terms!) in the smartly-converted front room of its proprietors, it has an exclusive air, making it perfect for whenever you want something particularly special.

Sala Thong
35 Newnham Road, 01223 323178

Sala Thong is a small, thriving Thai restaurant. It is tiny, which makes for intimacy, but can get very crowded. It is testament to the place that, after returning from backpacking in Thailand, this writer still can't get enough of the place! It offers both the usual fragrant, mouth-busting crowd pleasers as well as some subtler alternatives. It is definitely worth opting for a set menu (around £11 per head) but mixing and matching is always fun!

Trinity Vaults
Trinity Street

Newly refurbished to the tune of £1 million, Trinity Vaults lies in the cellars below Trinity Street. Once home to a Greek restaurant, the walls are now covered with modern art and house a slick, spacious and kookily-designed bar-restaurant that serves good food fashionably presented.

Venue
Regent Street, 01223 367333

In Cambridge terms, Venue is pretty young, having been opened just three years ago by Gary Curshen (who resembles a corpulent Jean Reno), who wanted to offer the dining public of Cambridge something very different. This is a sleek, chic, live jazz venue. It is refreshing that this establishment has forged a new path and not attempted, as so many have done previously, to ape the country house style that is so prevalent here in Cambridge. The cuisine is as original as the ink drawings that adorn the walls.

:student favourites

The Bengal
4 Fitzroy Street, 01223 351010

This vies with the Curry Queen (reviewed below) for best curry house in Cambridge. Marginally closer to town than its rival, it is located near to the Grafton Centre. It is slightly more expensive than other curry houses, but the extra is worth it for the dips and sauces that accompany many dishes. Reputed to be the curry house of choice for the Indian cricket team on their tours to Cambridge!

The Bun Shop
1 King's Street, 01223 366866

This pub is a three in one - downstairs a wine bar on one side and a real-ale pub on the other; upstairs a Spanish Tapas bar. The real ale bar serves traditional British pub food – from some of the biggest doorstep sandwiches in the history of pub grub to scampi and chips. Their Sunday lunches are highly recommended and come very reasonably priced. Some supervisors have even been known to hold supervisions here, and it's a particular favourite with Sidney students, most of whom live within a stone's throw of the pub.

The Curry Queen
Mill Road, 01223 351027

Ok, so this is miles away from the universe that is

the town centre (actually, Mill Road is about 15 minutes walk from the centre of the town), but it's worth it. In a street loaded with restaurants and curry houses, the Curry Queen still stands out as one of the top two curry houses in Cambridge. Pleasant service, great grub, curries to-die-for and a generous student discount make this restaurant a favourite undergraduate venue. They take bookings and can house large, rowdy parties, handling it all with a smile.

Footlights
Grafton Centre, 01223 323434

Footlights is a no-nonsense Mexican-American grill. You get exactly what you pay for, which is large portions of meat and cream and sauce, washed down with a pint, or, if you're feeling adventurous, a Corona with a slice of lime. The interior reminds one of a B-grade Zorro pastiche, but it is very cheerful (if not that cheap).

Garfunkels
21/24 Bridge Street, 01223 311053

Conveniently located and spacious, Garfunkels is pretty good news for the hungry of Cambridge. The menu offers a comprehensive selection of American-style food. Their mixed platters represent excellent value for money – large enough for even the biggest of rugby players.

Henry's
Quayside, 01223 324649

The riverside location and small al-fresco section makes this a pleasant place to grab a bite to eat. A large bar/restaurant offering a wide range of decent food at reasonable prices, Henry's (below) is popular with groups of students looking for a great brunch the morning after. It can get very full at weekends and on sunny summer days getting an outside table is difficult, but there are plenty of river-view tables inside.

No. 1 King's Parade
01223 359506

This well-established Cambridge venue is opposite King's College. That this restaurant is aimed at tourists is obvious from the moment one steps under the five-feet-high mural of Henry VIII on the way in. The restaurant is full of character, set in the ancient cellars of an old University building; it offers an intimate and relaxed mid-range dining experience.

Pierre Victoire
90-92 Regent Street, 01223 570170

This place has a French vibe and, as one of a large chain with restaurants in practically every town, is certainly somewhere most people will feel at home. The prices are great if you take advantage of the lunch time specials; also worth looking out for are the pre-theatre special deals: two courses for considerably less than a tenner.

Pizza Express
7a Jesus Lane, 01223 324033
or St. Andrew's Street, 01223 361320
Neither branch takes bookings.

One of the two links in the Pizza Express chain here in Cambridge deserves a special mention simply because of the location. '7a Jesus Lane' provides a relatively cheap tasty meal in tremendously elegant surroundings, and, being open till late, is a favourite with the casts of student shows at the nearby ADC Theatre, who often head round the corner to 7a for a post-show meal. Back when men were men and women couldn't study here, this place was part of the exclusive Pitt Club. Today, restaurant-goers can choose to dine in either the lighter marbled and mirrored dining room or the more grandiose book-cased drawing room. The atmosphere is enhanced by a light tinkling on the ivories of a grand piano in the hallway. While the St. Andrew's Street venue may not be so snazzy, it serves the same decent nosh and is perfectly pleasant, if more generic.

The Rainbow Vegetarian Bistro
9a King's Parade, 01223 321551

This small vegetarian restaurant, hidden in cellars opposite Kings, offers an eclectic, though fairly limited, range of dishes in friendly, unpretentious surroundings. The service is friendly and efficient. Considering the emphasis on fresh, organic food, the prices are fairly reasonable. Somehow, though, tasty as it all is, the servings are never quite enough to leave this writer feeling full.

Tatties
Sussex Street

If you're of celtic extraction you'll be way ahead on this one. Tatties – potatoes, in English – is a curio of Cambridge. Serving wholesome baked potatos with any combination of a huge number of exciting toppings; from the virtous to the vice-riddled, it is a favourite with students, particularly for Sunday brunches. Sandwiches, hot breakfasts, and a good selection of puddings also adorn the menu, but the tatties are the things to try.

Trattoria Pasta Fresca
66, Mill Road, 01223 352836

This unassuming restaurant appears at first glance to be one of Mill Road's many fast food takeaways, as the open kitchen is situated to the front of the restaurant and customers must pass beside it in order to access the seating area to the back. The fresh pasta and pizza is cooked in authentical Italian style, and provides the added entertainment of customers at thier tables being able to watch as the food is prepared. Word of mouth amongst students on this place is very strong, and the delicious food is served late into the night, making it a veritable favourite amongst undergraduates.

:coffee shops

In addition to the ubiquitous Starbucks, Costa Coffee et al, Cambridge has its very own funky coffee shop culture. Indigo – a haven of brightly coloured coffee shop cool tucked away on St. Edward's Passage near the Arts Theatre – offers fabulous coffees, amazing sandwiches and groovy atmosphere. It's a perfect place to hang, drink, flick through the papers and enjoy life. The only downside: the size. It's tiny – great for atmosphere but only for those quick off the mark!

If there is one hangout that is Cambridge it has to be Clowns. Italian-run and full of Italian flavour, this coffee shop offers tempestuous family antics, tasty homecooked pasta and tremendous tiramasu! The coffee is a cut above the chain-shop fayre and the surroundings are, well, surreal. The basic décor is enlivened by portraits of clowns drawn by artists aged from four to eighty-four adorning the walls.

Other cosmopolitan places for a coffee, croissant or a chat include Don Pasquale on Market Square (left) and Café Carrington on Market Street. Trockell, Ulmann and Freunde, on Pembroke Street, has a colourful bohemian atmosphere and serves delicious coffees, teas, croissants and cakes.

Martin's Coffee House at the end of Trumpington Street is another student favourite, usually crowded during termtime. Martin's is a popular refuge for students from the Architecture and History of Art faculties opposite, and is also the place to spot the journalists and politicians of the future – the Varsity and CUSU offices are practically next door.

:tea-shops

Afternoon tea is historically a uniquely English tradition, now exported worldwide. 'High tea', at a table piled high with sandwiches and cakes, has long been a favourite way to end an afternoon. Cambridge has a plethora of tea-shops, suitable for all tastes.

Auntie's Tea Shop, opposite Great St Mary's Church in St Mary's Passage, offers a full waitress service and a wide range of teas and cakes and can fill up during the summer. A quieter alternative is The Cambridge Tearoom on Wheeler Street, conveniently situated opposite the Tourist Information Office. The Rainbow Bistro, the excellent vegetarian and vegan restaurant in King's Parade, also sells full cream teas.

For those prepared to forgo the convenience of waitress service, the choice widens. Directly across King's Parade from King's College is The Copper Kettle (left). This is a popular student haunt, and an excellent place from which to watch people passing by the windows. Other self-service tea-shops include Belinda's on Trinity Street and the cellar of Eaden Lilley's Food Hall on Sussex Street.

Best of all the tea places around Cambridge, however, must be The Orchard Tea Garden in Grantchester (see walk, p.73). Serving a wide range of teas and cakes, and also light lunches, seating is available not only inside but also outside in the extensive orchard on comfortable deck-chairs. The atmosphere seems to invite the visitor to spend the whole afternoon lounging around, and is reminiscent of the days when Virginia Woolf and Wittgenstein took tea in the same place. For those lucky enough to catch one, student plays are sometimes put on here in the open air during the summer vacation.

:fast food

Cambridge has its fair share of the inescapable fast food joints. These include Burger King (St. Andrew's Street), Pizza Hut, on Regent Street, and McDonald's on Rose Crescent (complete with mock-Classical 'ruins' inside).

However, there are some fast-food outlets with a great deal more character. Most popular with students, especially late at night, is The Gardenia Restaurant (affectionately known as 'Gardies') in Rose Crescent. This place corners the 3am market! Whilst the usual burgers (including great veggie options) and pizzas are available, Gardies is a Greek restaurant offering great kebabs, falafel and salad-filled pitta breads. Few students make it through their time at Cambridge without regular trips to 'Gardies'.

Other places to grab fast food in the daytime are from the burger and hot dog stands on Sidney Street and Fitzroy Street, and the baked potato stand on Market Square. After dark, the 'Van of Life' on Market Square offers great grub. Their veggie hotdogs are mouthwatering enough to turn even the most staunch carnivore!

:pubs

One of Cambridge's largest pubs, and one that every student knows, is the Anchor on Silver Street (background picture), opposite Queens' College. Inside, drinkers can enjoy a pint on any of the pub's three levels, the lowest of which is often loud and packed in the evenings. Outside, there is a terrace over the Cam, with space for punts to tie up nearby.

Just across the road is the Mill, well known for its wide range of well-kept 'real ales', and ferociously strong organic scrumpy. Take a look at the blackboard behind the bar to find out which beers are in. A wide range of fruit wines are also stocked. The Mill is particularly pleasant in the summer, when it is possible to take a drink out onto Sheep's Green, the green space opposite, close to the river. Many students choose this pub to celebrate the end of their exams. If you are drinking outside, remember to ask for a plastic glass.

The Granta, on Newnham Road, next to the Mill Pond, is a large, modern, split-level pub with terraces overlooking the river.

THE ANCHOR

A little further along the river is the Fort St. George, which until the 17th century stood on an island in the middle of the Cam. It is now firmly attached to the banks, on the edge of Midsummer Common. The food is good, and barbecues are held on the terrace in the summer.

The Boat House, on Chesterton Road, has plenty of seating outside and in, and it is a good place to watch college boat crews plying up and down the river in term time.

Away from the river, in the city centre, stands the Eagle, adopted by Corpus students as their college pub. Cambridge was once even more full of inns and hostelries, as it was a major trading centre and inland port, and there was great demand for lodgings, stables, refreshment and entertainment for travellers passing through. The Eagle is one of the few places which retains its courtyard, where coaches would pull in to change horses and pick up passengers. The pub was also a favourite with air pilots in the Second World War, a fact which is reflected in the signatures covering the roof of the aptly-named Air Force Bar. Fighter and bomber pilots from the nearby airfields would go to The Eagle to relax, and signed their names, or that of their squadron, on the ceiling. Whilst the Eagle is sometimes packed, and is more expensive than some of its competitors, it is definitely worth a visit. It is open all day, and serves food.

BARON OF BEEF
NEW
MENU

The Mitre and the Baron of Beef (previous page) stand next door to each other on Bridge Street. Both are regular haunts for students from neighbouring St. John's College. The Mitre is mid-sized and full of dark oak and candles, with good value bar food: a popular place to be at lunchtime. The Baron of Beef has a very traditional atmosphere, with a good set of regulars.

Just across Magdalene Bridge and right opposite Magdalene College is the Pickerel Inn. This was once the alternative bar for Magdalene, and time was when every other drinker sported a college scarf or blazer. Things have changed, however, and today the pub is a pleasant retreat for town, gown and tourists alike.

The Maypole, near Jesus Green on Park Street, does an excellent line in cocktails. The pub is well-known amongst students for being popular with the University acting community, as it is very close to the ADC Theatre.

King Street is famous for its pub crawl – known as the 'King Street Run' – which involved downing a pint in each of the many pubs along its length. This short street still boasts a fair number of pubs, each with very distinct personalities. The Champion of the Thames is as traditional as they come. The tiny St. Radegund, is fabulous fun. The landlord takes pleasure in abusing his guests and the pub grub extends to pistachio nuts served in a beaker! The King Street Run is part-pub, part-theme park and is worth a look in. The King street pubs are particularly popular with Sidney and Jesus students, as both colleges back onto this street.

If you are prepared to go a little out of the centre of Cambridge, there are a handful of excellent pubs which merit the walk. The Free Press in Prospect Row, behind the Police Station on the far side of Parker's Piece, is a hidden treasure. Quiet, with superbly-kept real ales and log fires and candles in the winter, it also serves good food. Watch out for the rabbits in the backyard garden, and the smallest 'snug' in Cambridge. Please note that it is a smoke-free pub.

Both the Clarendon Arms, in Clarendon Street (again, near Parker's Piece), and the Panton Arms, in Panton Street (off Lensfield Road), serve large, economically-priced traditional English Sunday roasts. The Clarendon is a particular favourite with students from nearby Emmanuel College. Further afield, The Live and Let Live, on the corner of Mawson Road and Cross Street, has a cosy, local atmosphere without being hostile.

At Wilbury's Cocktail Bar, proprietors David and Al are a class act. Warm, welcoming and thoroughly unpretentious, it serves the finest cocktails in town and at surprisingly low prices. Nearly all are just £3 apiece. David and Al genuinely love their business, and one of the pair is generally on hand to guide you through the copious menu, or even to mix something to your own specifications. Plans are afoot to open on Sunday nights with the added inducement of live jazz.

tourist information

tourist information

Cambridge Tourist Information Centre
Wheeler Street,
01223 322640

Gives details of tours, including private group tours, as well as lots of useful information for the tourist. Please note that any group of ten or more persons wishing to visit the colleges must be accompanied by a blue-badged Cambridge guide.

Ely
Oliver Cromwell House, 29 St. Mary's Street, 01353 662062

Huntingdon
c/o Library, Princes Street, 01480 425831

Saffron Walden
1 Market Place, Market Square, 01799 524282

Peterborough
45 Bridge Street, 01733 317336

hotels

Accommodation in Cambridge is usually difficult to find during the peak summer season, especially during 'May Week', (mid-June), around Graduation Day (late June/early July), and during the Cambridge festivals (late July). As a rule, it is wise to book well in advance.

This is by no means an exhaustive list of Cambridge's hotels, and inclusion does not imply our recommendation. More details of this and other types of accommodation, such as the YHA and YMCA, are available from the Tourist Information Office on Wheeler Street, which will also make reservations for you. Prices are intended only as a guide. Most hotels include the price of a full English breakfast in the room price.

hotels

Arundel House Hotel
53 Chesterton Road, 01223 367701
Single £39-£59, Double £55-£79

Garden House Hotel
Granta Place, 01223 259988
Single £110, double £145

Gonville Hotel (Best Western)
Gonville Place, 01223 366611
Single £77, Double £96

Crowne Plaza
Downing Street, 01223 464466
Single £76, double £96

Regent Hotel
41 Regent Street, 01223 351470
Single £59.50, double £79.50

Royal Cambridge Hotel
Trumpington Street, 01223 351631
Single £75, double £87.50

University Arms Hotel
Regent Street, 01223 351241
Single £95, Double £115

travel

by air:

Cambridge Airport
Newmarket Road, 01223 61133

Air taxi service: contact Cecil Aviation, 01223 294218

Tours and charter flights: Magnet Air Services, 01223 293621

Stansted Airport
Offers a wide variety of national and international flights.
01279 662379 or 01279 662520 for information.
The airport is approximately 30 minutes' drive from Cambridge, south along the M11, or an easy train journey from Cambridge Railway Station.

by rail:

Cambridge Railway Station
For national rail enquiries: 08457 484950
or www.railtrack.co.uk

by bus:

Cambridge Coach Station
Drummer Street
Intercity buses – National Express: 01223 460711
or www.gobycoach.com
Cambridge Coach Services: 01223 236333
Local buses (Cambus): 01223 423554

by car:

Children's car seats can be booked from those marked (c)

Avis Rent-a-Car, 245 Mill Road, 01223 212551 (c)

Budget Rent-a-Car, 303-5 Newmarket Road, 01223 323838

CamKars Hire, 362 Milton Road, 01223 425706

Hertz Rent-a-Car, Barnwell Road, 01223 416634

Kenning Car Hire, 47 Coldham's Lane, 01223 361538 (c)

car parking:

Warning: parking in central Cambridge can be extremely difficult. Do not park illegally (on yellow lines or elsewhere), or there is a risk that your car will be removed without notice. The current fee for removal is over £100.

Short Stay:	Lion Yard (Downing Street) Park Street Grafton Centre (Maid's Causeway/ East Road)
Long Stay:	Gonville Place Saxon Street Gold Street
Coach Park:	City Football Ground, Milton Road

Park and Ride facilities are also available for the city.

by taxi:

There are taxi ranks on St. Andrew's Street, by the Bus Station on Drummer Street, and at the Railway Station.

help and advice

Emergency:
Dial 999 and ask for Ambulance, Fire or Police.

Hospital:
Addenbrooke's Hospital, Hills Road, 01223 245151

Chemists:
Boots, 28 Petty Cury and 65 Sidney Street, 01223 350213
Coulson Horace and Sons, 66 Bridge Street, 01223 353002
Lloyd's Chemist, 30 Trumpington Street, 01223 359449

Phone Line Services:
Citizen's Advice Bureau, 01223 353875
Samaritans, 01223 364455 (24 hour)
Rape Crisis, 01223 358314 (24 hour)

Post Offices:
9-11 St Andrew's Street (Main Post Office, last collection Mon-Fri 7.45pm) 01223 323325
23-24 Trinity Street
2a Trumpington Street

Lion Yard Shops 50 yds
Public Library 100
Toilets &
Magistrates Court
Lion Yard Car Park 125yds
Park & Ride
Bus Stop
275yds
Grafton
Shopping Centre
½ m

contributors

Writers: Steve Bennett, Phillip Breen, Sophie Craig, Rachel Flowerday, Ben Horslen, Sophie Levy, Abi McLoughlin, Dan Moore, Madelaine Savage, Claude Schneider

Photographers: Steve Bennett, Pete Le May, Abi McLoughlin, Claude Schneider

Editorial Assistant: Abi McLoughlin

Thanks also to Tim Harris, Ken Barnett and Origen Production Ltd, Diana Tapp, Dr. Michael Franklin, Kate Norgrove, all at Varsity, the cast and crew of Memoirs of a Dead Man, and Cambridge University Press for kindly permitting the use of their map of Cambridge

Credit is also due to past editors of and contributors to the three earlier editions of Cambridge Through Student Eyes, without whose work this guide would not be possible.

the end